The Project Management Mindset

The Project Management Mindset

Think like a Project Manager

Ian Juniper

ISBN: 978-1-0685330-0-6

Cover design by Maui Waui Design mauiwauidesign.co.uk

To those seeking to make change that matters, and who think a little differently

Table of Contents

Preface   1

The Foundations

 1 - Projects, Management, and Managers   8

 2 A Brief History of Change   24

The Principles

 3 People Before Processes   38

 4 The Three Roles of the Project Manager   49

The Mindset Tips

The Consultant

 5 Know Your Customer and Why They Hired You   62

 6 Projects Don't Fail, Project Managers Do   70

 7 Maintain a Self-Employed Mindset   83

The Planner

 8 Create Problems, Deliver Solutions   94

 9 Own Nothing, and Keep Your Customer Happy   101

The Leader

 10 The Confidence Game   110

 11 Protect, Serve, and Challenge   118

General

 12 Build Your Customer's House   133

 13 Programmes Are Just Really Big Projects   142

Final Thoughts   150

References   156

Acknowledgements and Thanks   159

About the Author   160

Index   161

Preface

Being a Project Manager requires more than simply knowing how to manage projects.

That may seem like a contradictory statement, so let me explain. Project Management is an art form being treated as a science, and when teaching Project Management we tend to focus solely on the science. A new Project Manager will begin their career by learning one of the many recognised methodologies along with its associated terminology, processes, tools, and documentation, everything a new Project Manager should need to shepherd a project on its journey to completion. But I believe it misses the most important part: the art of being a Project Manager.

Project Management is simple in theory, while in practice, it's complex. Over time, the way we have approached it has added to that complexity, and this additional complexity poses a significant problem for both Project Managers and the organisations trying to make meaningful change. In the pursuit of projects without pain, we have over-engineered things in a manner that complicates as much as it simplifies. We've developed an overly prescriptive approach that detracts as much as it adds. And we've bought into a belief that if we follow a series of pre-determined, standardised steps, we'll achieve a pre-determined standard of outcome. In my experience, this is rarely the case.

Project Managers are expected to navigate a team through these steps to achieve a desired outcome. To help them perform this level of coordination, they learn one of many methodologies and achieve an accredited qualification. In parallel, businesses requiring change adopt a specific methodology as their standard, organisation-wide approach for their projects.

A cursory online search suggests that at the time of publishing this book, there are somewhere in the region of three million people certified with one of the four major project management institutes: International Project Management Association (IPMA), Institute of Project Management (IPM), Project Management Institute (PMI), and PRINCE2. Aligned with these are numerous organisations across the world adopting them in some form as their standard change methodology. These statistics alone suggest a high rate of project satisfaction and delivery proficiency within these organisations. But having worked within and led projects for 20 years across organisations of different sizes, industries, locations, and cultures, my experience is that most still have a negative perception of their project experiences. I would also suggest that many Project Managers have a negative perception of projects they have led within those organisations.

For organisations, 'project pain' means additional cost. Delay requires more resource or requires resources for longer. It carries an opportunity cost in the form of possible delayed revenue or the blockage of other important initiatives. Projects may impact an organisation's operations more severely than originally expected and possibly for longer. The morale of individuals involved may be negatively impacted, and there is a wide range of other potentially negative consequences.

For Project Managers, the personal impact can be equally problematic. A Project Manager's reputation is directly correlated to the success of the projects they deliver. Or more accurately, and even more concerning, to the perceived success of a project. Over time, the 'wading through treacle' or 'herding cats' that many Project Managers experience can deplete their enthusiasm and confidence; in turn, this can lead to a negative perception of the profession.

The reality is that change, by definition, requires some discomfort and inconvenience. Most of us have experienced the pain of moving house at some point in our lives, and I doubt many would describe it as a positive time. We accept that long-term benefit requires some level of time, effort, cost, and inconvenience. Hurt now and feel good later, if you will. But it shouldn't be unnecessarily painful. Done well, the level of disruption and inconvenience you are forced to endure should be on par with expectation. It shouldn't cost more, take longer, or require more effort than you expected. The same is true for larger-scale projects.

So why, with well-established methodologies in circulation and a deep pool of trained and certified Project Managers, do so many projects experience so much unnecessary pain? Over time, why haven't these multiple methodologies overcome the common issues encountered by so many projects? The answer to these questions is not that the individual methodologies per se are the problem. I have certified in PRINCE2, trained in Six Sigma, and worked extensively with Agile and Scrum, among many other flavours (see *Chapter 2* for more information on these). And while I believe they have had a significantly positive impact on the landscape of change, I do think they have inadvertently introduced a problem. Not through their inherent nature, or the solutions they each offer, but through the industry they have created and the mentality they instil. I believe they have driven an increasingly dogmatic approach where methodologies themselves are the sole solution to organisational challenges. New trends have swept through industries at pace, with new and 'hybrid' methodologies emerging, yet the age-old process of 'getting stuff done' persists. And I believe that's because the method isn't the problem, and methodologies aren't the solution.

Rather, I believe the answer lies in what methodologies don't or can't teach. That Project Management is an art form being treated as a science. That there is more to successful project delivery than following a series of defined steps. That instead of focusing solely on how projects are managed, we should focus on developing great Project Managers. In other words, we should help Project Managers master the skills and behaviours they need to navigate the dynamic environment of a changing organisation. People skills to manage the challenge and expectations that senior leadership places upon a team of technical experts executing complex tasks. And behaviours that enable Project Managers to maintain order within chaos and be a calm force in times of turbulence.

The Project Management Mindset aims to teach the 'art' of Project Management. To help individuals think like a Project Manager and build mental agility to help identify and avoid the numerous challenges they face, along with the resilience to manage the expectations placed upon them. It seeks to develop the soft skills and competencies a Project Manager requires to establish and maintain the fundamental conditions for project success.

And to do this, it focuses on two core principles:

1. **People are more important than processes**

2. **A Project Manager has three roles, not one**

The book's 13 chapters are organised into 3 distinct sections.

- **The Foundations**
  A simple overview of Project Management for those new to the subject
- **The Principles**
  Introducing the theory of 'People before Processes' and the three roles of the Project Manager
- **The Mindset Tips**
  A series of tips to help establish the mindset required to understand the three roles of the Project Manager and how to perform them well

This book is not intended to replace Project Management methodologies but to complement them, to teach the 'art' of Project Management and complement the 'science'. It doesn't teach how to perform specific tasks that need to be completed within a project, such as creating a plan or how to use specific tools. Individual methodologies cover these specifics within their curriculum. While methodologies teach you how to manage a project, this book will teach you how to think like a Project Manager.

And finally, this book aims to frame the issues simply, tangibly, and in a way that is memorable. It isn't intended to be in any way disrespectful to the profession, the industry, organisations, or individuals. Rather, it is intended to be engaging, to provoke thought, and hopefully bring clarity to those learning the profession.

I hope you find the book useful and that it helps you enjoy delivering change as much as I do.

The Foundations

Chapter 1

Projects, Management, and Managers

To start our journey into the art of Project Management, we're going to cover the fundamentals. And at the risk of 'teaching Granny to suck eggs', these fundamentals set a foundation of knowledge that makes learning and practising Project Management simple. And even if you are familiar with Project Management, it's worth spending a moment to review the basics as you may benefit from looking at things from a different perspective.

To begin, we need to understand what Project Management is. And to do this, we need to understand four simple concepts.

1. What we mean by Projects, Project Management, and Project Managers

2. The 'stages' of a project

3. Why delivering in stages is important

4. The roles and responsibilities within the project

Let's dive into each one.

Concept 1: What do we mean by Projects, Project Management, and Project Managers?

Projects

What is a project? This may be a clichéd question that's addressed in any piece of Project Management training you'll encounter, but we also need to address it here, and for good reason. The fact that the question is asked and addressed so frequently demonstrates how much confusion there is, even at the very basic level. And by continuously needing to re-affirm our understanding of what a project is, we prove this lack of understanding.

The answers from some of the industry bodies aren't necessarily consistent. Take the following examples (at the time of publishing):

> "A project is a temporary venture that exists to produce a defined outcome that leads to the achievement of intended benefits (value). Each project will have agreed and unique objectives as well as its own budget, schedule, deliverables (products) and tasks. A project typically involves people from different parts of an organization who are brought together to accomplish a specific goal."
>
> **PRINCE2/AXELOS**

Alternatively:

> "A project is a temporary endeavour undertaken to create a unique product, service, or result."
>
> **Project Management Institute**

And finally:

> "A project is a unique, transient endeavour, undertaken to achieve planned objectives, which

You'll notice that the common themes are around the temporary nature of a project and aiming to achieve a common output. For simplicity, I'd summarise this as:

"A specific series of tasks performed to achieve an expected one-time result."

For a new Project Manager, the important thing to understand is that projects are disruptive efforts performed to 'move the needle' – things that require sacrifice and effort in the short term so that we benefit in the long term. They are not a series of repeated steps taken to achieve something (i.e. a process). If you need help visualising this, think moving house, building a house, landscaping a garden, or converting a camper van! All of these require a dedicated, additional effort to change something from the way it is today to the way it's needed for the future.

Project Management

If Projects are what we do, Project Management is how we do it. Looking at the same sources, Project Management is defined as follows:

initiate, plan, execute and manage the way that new initiatives or changes are implemented within an organization."

PRINCE2/AXELOS

And:

"Project management is the application of knowledge, skills, tools, and techniques to project activities to meet project requirements. It's the practice of planning, organizing, and executing the tasks needed to turn a brilliant idea into a tangible product, service, or deliverable."

Project Management Institute

And finally:

"Project management is the application of processes, methods, skills, knowledge and experience to achieve specific project objectives according to the project acceptance criteria within agreed parameters. Project management has final deliverables that are constrained to a finite timescale and budget."

Association for Project Management

All of these are actually pretty good. The key themes in this instance are around a series of skills, processes, and tools to help projects achieve their intended outcomes. The other key theme is being within agreed parameters. Again, this can be simplified; and I would summarise it simply as:

"Project Management is the practice of delivering projects in a controlled fashion to maximise the probability of achieving the outcomes."

I'm tempted to include the use of processes, tools, skills, and so on in my definition, but I think that falls into 'how' rather than 'what' Project Management is. The parameters referred to in the APM definition generally mean the time, costs, and quality expected, and generally, I agree. But focusing too much on parameters such as these can sometimes be at the cost of other factors that are better drivers of good Project Management. Which is why I prefer the term 'in a controlled fashion'.

The Project Manager
The definitions here are slightly simpler. **PRINCE2** generally doesn't define the term. While we have:

> "Project managers are organized, goal-oriented professionals who use innovation, creativity, and collaboration to lead projects that make an impact."
>
> **Project Management Institute**

And then:

> "The individual responsible for the successful delivery of the project."
>
> **Association for Project Management**

Of the two, I think the APM definition is as simple and effective as it can be. My only caveat would be around the definition of the word 'successfully'. But we'll touch on that later in the book.

Concept 2: The stages of a Project

Project Management methodologies focus on how to manage projects in controlled stages through the entire life cycle of a project. As processes, they define a series of steps a Project Manager (and project team) should follow to maximise the chances of a desired outcome with control and efficiency. The associated tools and techniques support those involved to collaborate and obtain what they require during the process.

While there are differences between the various methodologies, they tend to break a project down into five general stages.

1. **Project Initiation**
   Where the general concept of the idea is formed, a Business Case (why we should run the project) is prepared, outcomes are defined, and strategy is proposed.

The proposal is assessed for viability and packaged ready for an investment decision to proceed to the next stage.

2. **Planning**

   Where the original concept is expanded in more detail. Resource and budget requirements are defined, deliverables are identified, and initial planning is performed. Agreement on how to manage and govern the project occurs.

3. **Execution**

   Where the plan is executed by the project team in pre-agreed stages. This is overseen by the Customer and an Oversight Group to ensure the project remains true to its ambition, timelines, budget, and specification.

4. **Monitoring**

   A stage that runs in parallel with the Execution (I would argue it isn't distinct from it) that focuses on monitoring the execution of the project itself. Provides confidence in execution against time, budget, and quality of deliverables.

5. **Closure**

   Where agreement to close the project is sought and project deliverables are handed over. Where the Project Manager disbands the project team and provides an opportunity for feedback and learning for future projects.

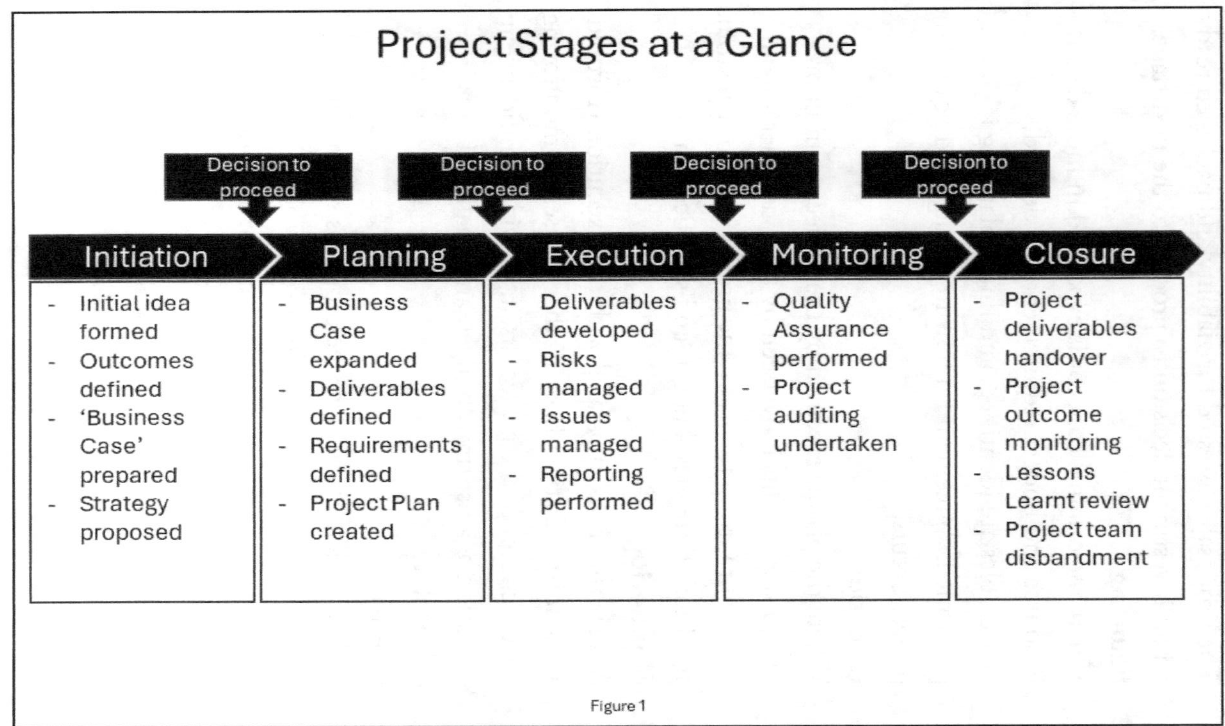

Figure 1

A Project Manager is hired to manage each of these stages and does so under the guidance of the Customer and the Oversight Group assigned to ensure the project delivers its outcomes. Various tasks are set to be completed in these stages, with associated tools and documents aligned in support. At the beginning of each stage, the detailed tasks to be executed and the closure criteria are proposed. Both are agreed by the Customer and then executed. Status updates are given throughout the stage to give visibility of progress, and at the end of the stage, formal closure is requested based on the agreed closure criteria. This process is then repeated until the project is completed.

The sub-stage variance

There is a slight variance in this process within the Execution stage, which is broken into several sub-stages. These are agreed upon ahead of delivering them, in the form of high-level milestones: key points in the delivery journey at which something significant is expected to be delivered. Each of these is approached individually as a full stage would be, with a detailed plan created and closure criteria agreed, and the process is repeated for each sub-stage. Some details are forecast for future sub-stages, and the closer each one is to the current point in time, the more detail is added. That's not to say the Project Manager doesn't think about things further down the road, but the level of detail, and the frequency of visiting that detail, is far less than the current sub-stage.

So, for each sub-stage in a project, we fully detail:

- The things that are going to be delivered
- The tasks needed to deliver them
- Who needs to perform those tasks
- When those tasks need to be performed
- How we agree that the things delivered are correct
- Who agrees that the things delivered are correct
- The boundaries to operate within without having to report back

Once this is detailed, approval is sought before proceeding. The plan is then executed, progress is reported as agreed, then 'rinsed and repeated'. The final update to the Customer that closes one sub-stage also presents the plan for the next. This effectively breaks up the execution of a large project with a very wide set of outcomes into a series of digestible, manageable deliverables.

Concept 3: Why delivering in stages is important

The purpose of the staged approach is to provide control. Given that projects are generally complex, long-term, and come at significant cost, the consequences of overrun can be significant, and the viability of the project may not be guaranteed throughout.

To put this into a recent context, a project to build a new office before the 2020 Covid pandemic might have made great business sense for a fast-growing organisation. Two years later, with remote or hybrid working becoming the norm, that project might seem somewhat less appealing, even if some money and effort had been spent already. Continuing to sink funds and effort into an initiative that is unlikely to provide benefit would be unwise, to say the least. A wiser choice would be to cut potential losses, re-use the work already developed (wherever possible) and allocate the resources to an initiative with a greater chance of providing benefits.

Concept 4: Roles and responsibilities within the project

To effectively manage the project, several roles need to be filled. While these roles obviously need to be filled for the project to run, it is critical that those involved (particularly the Project Manager) understand why the roles are needed and how to perform them.

The table below details the key roles and responsibilities, together with some practical examples to help highlight how the roles should be performed. Most methodologies tend to overcomplicate the naming of these roles. I prefer to keep them simple, clear, and effective.

Project Role	Expected Behaviour	Examples
The Customer (commonly called the Sponsor or Executive)	Demands delivery of outcomes Makes key project decisions Removes roadblocks	'Prove to me we are on track' 'Tell me what you need' 'What needs to happen?'
The Oversight Group (commonly called a Steering Committee)	Supports project Customer Approves operational changes Manages operational challenges	'Tell me how my operation will be impacted' 'Convince me my operation won't fall over' 'Tell me how my team can help'
Project Manager	Responsible for managing the project through the project stages Plans and executes the project within agreed parameters Proposes	'What activities get us to our objectives?' 'Where are we against plan?' 'What issues do you need help with?'

	governance structure for project and updates accordingly throughout	'Tell me what you think could go wrong' 'This is where we are with the project'
Workstream Lead	Responsible for specific deliverables or groups of deliverables within the project Provides expertise on a specific outcome Manages SMEs (see below) within the workstream	'This is how I intend to deliver this outcome' 'This is what I need to do it' 'This is when I think it can be done'
Subject Matter Expert (SME)	Delivers specific activity within the project workstreams Provides specific expertise to the project and workstream lead	'This is the best way to achieve the outcome' 'I think this task can be done within X days'

| | Advises on best option to deliver workstream outcomes | 'Have we also considered …?' |

The Workstream Lead and Subject Matter Experts may be new concepts if you are new to Project Management, but they are quite simple to understand. Generally, a project plan is divided logically into groups, or workstreams. This is a way of grouping activity and deliverables together for ease of governance. Each workstream is headed by a workstream lead, who is responsible for managing those deliverables and the people delivering them. Common examples are grouping financial activities into a workstream or combining Human Resources and People activities. Operations, communications, marketing, each one of these could be led by an empowered representative who understands the subject matter and has the presence and authority to drive that activity.

Within each workstream, Subject Matter Experts provide support with their expertise. They make up part of the project team and perform the tasks required to produce the deliverables. Grouping allows for a delegated management structure and clear visibility for oversight. While the project stages (and sub-stages) allow the overall project to be divided up into manageable pieces, the workstreams allow the tasks and the team to be similarly organised. The Project Manager can work closely with a smaller 'core' team of workstream leads, and each workstream lead can work with the SMEs in their workstream to deliver the tasks required.

The last part we'll cover here is the Oversight Group. In most methodologies it's referred to as a Steering Committee, or 'SteerCo'. This is a group of individuals who can offer meaningful support and insight to the Customer and/or who have a vested interest in the project itself. A classic example is a finance representative. They will have a vested interest in ensuring the project is delivered within the approved budget and be keen to ensure the project delivers on its outcomes, particularly any financial benefits. They may also be needed during the project to approve financial decisions or provide insight to the project team.

In Conclusion

There are many project management methodologies and definitions out there. This in itself can lead to confusion. But understanding the fundamentals outlined in this chapter can make learning and practising Project Management simple. It can also help lay some key foundations, as the following chapters will demonstrate.

Chapter 2

A Brief History of Change

As we have discovered, the sheer number of methodologies related to organisational change can be quite daunting for new Project Managers. Over recent decades, changes to communications, technology, and working patterns have seen an explosion in new methods to address the perceived challenges they bring. I remain unconvinced that all these new methodologies are needed or that some of them are actually useful.

Understanding the purpose of the different methodologies, as well as the context in which they were developed, can serve as an important base for a Project Manager's core knowledge. Having a full toolbox to choose from and knowing what each tool is for will help you select the right one for the job. Let's take a look at some historical timelines and build an understanding of what's out there and why.

The Second Industrial Revolution – a focus on production

The history of operational improvement and change is long and complicated. For me, the era most relevant to modern business began in the early 1900s with Taylor's *The Principles of Scientific Management* and Henry Ford's moving assembly line. These approaches came in a period that introduced mass manufacturing of products and a focus on how to increase productivity, including a more scientific approach to production methods and task specialisation. It moved away from all workers doing all things to selected workers doing specialised things in sequence – and so producing a final output more quickly. It brought the work to the worker, allowing them to focus on becoming excellent at a few specific jobs and repeating those in quick succession.

The social impacts of this innovation cannot be understated. Not only did it eventually lead to a reduction in the price of the Ford Model T (by more than half), but it also significantly altered the way labour was managed in terms of payment, profit share, and shift working for 24-hour production. A true manufacturing revolution.

Getting Lean – Just in Time

By the 1950s, the focus was shifting from this type of mass production. While hugely successful, it presented a logistical challenge because of the large volumes of materials needed to manufacture units based on anticipated demand. This required significant storage space and also limited the variety of products that could be produced. During this time, the Japanese (in what would become the Toyota Motor Company) started exploring the possibility of producing products to meet actual demand – in terms of both volume and the ability to vary the manufacturing process to produce different products. It achieved this by supplying people with materials the moment they were needed rather than storing them for future use. A 'pull' rather than a 'push' method that came to be known as 'Just-in-Time' manufacturing. This method, which would eventually be labelled as the Toyota Production System, drove significant efficiency into manufacturing and introduced the concept of continuous improvement of processes. This established the Japanese as the powerhouse of manufacturing and innovation we know today, and it set the tone for manufacturing for decades to follow.

The focus on quality

Overlapping the focus on lean manufacturing, organisations started to face challenges around improvements in technology, particularly in the field of electrical engineering. Japan's ability to produce quality goods at a reasonable cost – both consumer and commercial – saw large Western industrial nations falling behind. Consumer confidence in Japanese electrical goods led to a seismic shift in importing from overseas rather than buying locally produced, more expensive, less reliable products.

This saw many large corporations making organisational adjustments to focus on quality, spawning methodologies such as Total Quality Management (TQM) and Six Sigma, introduced around the 1980s and early 1990s. These focused on a few key concepts, notably making customer need the key driver for business outcomes and an organisation-wide focus and accountability for quality control. They introduced statistical measurement and analysis to monitor and prove the quality of products. The American corporation General Electric adopted Six Sigma as a central business methodology, becoming one of the largest global corporations in existence and attributing their significant cost-saving results to its implementation. This success led to Six Sigma being widely adopted across Western organisations.

Waterfall and Agile

Alongside these shifts in manufacturing, from the 1950s onwards, the field of software engineering was developing, and in the 1970s and 1980s, the waterfall method of development was formed. This focused on developing software in stages (analysis, design, construction, testing, deployment, maintenance), with each phase performed sequentially. As the Information Technology revolution continued, the waterfall method became the default approach to development within global industry. With the introduction of client/server infrastructure, particularly the internet, global collaboration became possible.

Through the 1990s, global organisations capitalised on this capability by outsourcing software development to countries abundant with software development skills and a lower cost of living, and so benefitted from wage arbitrage. Initially this was financially successful, but the 'disconnect' introduced by the distances involved proved somewhat incompatible with the waterfall method. Local teams were creating specifications and designing software to be sent thousands of miles away – to be built by a completely separate team, people they were unlikely to have ever met. These gaps in time, distance, and communication impacted quality and led to a growing frustration and, eventually, to the search for a new approach.

In stepped the Agile Manifesto, an approach developed by a group of programming and development experts collectively known as The Agile Alliance. The Agile Manifesto proposed a set of values which suggested a more iterative and collaborative approach to software development. It focused on developing functional software alongside the end customer, adapting throughout the development processes rather than following a rigid plan. This was commonly combined with an already existing method known as Scrum, which helps Agile teams provide oversight and governance to their development without it becoming overly burdensome.

And in the background, Project Management
In parallel with these activities, Project Management was developing. The initial pin on the map was the creation of the Gantt Chart by Henry Gantt in around 1915. Interestingly, Henry Gantt was once an assistant to Frederick W. Taylor, author of *The Principles of Scientific Management* referenced earlier. The Gantt Chart was developed to enable the visual tracking of scheduled tasks, showing progress against a plan. It detailed dependencies between tasks, showing activities that couldn't start or finish until other tasks had started or finished.

The discipline of scheduling tasks and estimating costs was (and still is) significantly important within large-scale development activity. Civil engineering, construction, and defence organisations were the primary proponents of early Project Management, where the sheer amount of labour and materials involved in large-scale projects made any issues with scheduling disproportionately costly. The most notable early example was the construction of the Hoover Dam, which was completed in 1935 – a project so large, employing so many workers, that it required the construction of its own city, a sizeable project in itself, just to house the workers.

Project Management was further developed through the 1950s with the development of the Critical Path Method (CPM), a method focused on predicting project duration by sequencing the tasks critical for completing the project, how they linked with other tasks in the sequence, and their estimated duration. This provided the ability to visually map the route through the various tasks that were critical for the project to progress and complete on time. Effectively, it produced a view of the primary tasks within a project that could not be moved without altering timelines, as opposed to secondary tasks that had more flexibility.

At the same time, the Program Evaluation and Review Technique (PERT) was developed by Charles E. Clark for the US Navy. Similar to CPM, it provided an approach to estimating the scheduling of tasks using statistical analysis. Specifically, it made estimates using four 'time types': optimistic, pessimistic, most likely, and expected.

In the 1960s, both the International Project Management Association (IPMA, at the time called the IMSA) and Project Management Institute (PMI) were launched to solidify Project Management as a profession and to bring together common aspects utilised in different industries. This led to the next significant milestone, the publication of the Project Management Body of Knowledge (PMBOK) Guide, published by PMI in the mid-1990s. This guide was the first notable document to bring together a variety of knowledge, methodologies, and practices around Project Management. I would argue it was the first example of a move towards a standard Project Management methodology. At the time of writing, it is in its seventh edition. Around the same time as the publication of the first PMBOK Guide, the Projects In Controlled Environments (PRINCE) methodology was published, soon followed by PRINCE2 in 1996.

The history of Project Management shows how it has continuously advanced to address the challenge of delivering complex, high-risk outcomes. To provide visibility around what tasks are required to deliver an outcome, how long those tasks might take, and in which order they need to be performed. Where logistical challenges have had the potential to cause significant (sometimes catastrophic) problems, Project Management has helped to simplify the view of the route to delivery.

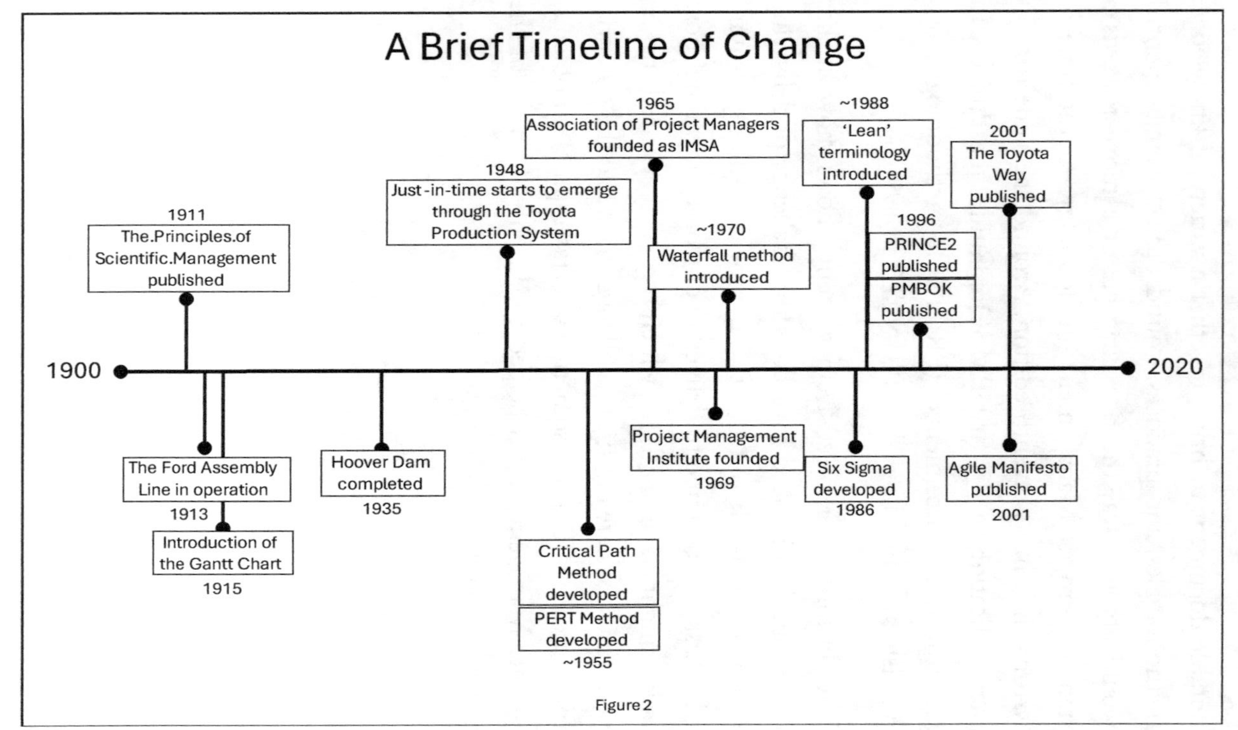

A Brief Timeline of Change
1911
The.Principles.of Scientific.Management published
1948
Just-in-time starts to emerge through the Toyota Production System
1965
Association of Project Managers founded as IMSA
~1970
Waterfall method introduced
~1988
'Lean' terminology introduced
1996
PRINCE2 published
PMBOK published
2001
The Toyota Way published
1900
2020
The Ford Assembly Line in operation
1913
Introduction of the Gantt Chart
1915
Hoover Dam completed
1935
Critical Path Method developed
PERT Method developed
~1955
Project Management Institute founded
1969
Six Sigma developed
1986
Agile Manifesto published
2001
Figure 2

Figure 2

A long, detailed history, but so what?
While a historical summary of the methodologies might be interesting, the real question is how does it help? Well, it's important to understand both the environment in which the methodologies were introduced and the challenges they were introduced to overcome.

Awareness of context and history can help you choose the right tool for the right job, helping avoid the confusion that has been introduced by the growth of numerous hybrid methodologies, however well-intentioned they may be. Without a compelling reason to exist or an environmental challenge to solve, I would question whether some of these are actually needed. Indeed, fewer and more concise methodologies may be the best way forward.

Figure 3 gives a simple summary of the categories of methodology and some examples that sit within them.

The Change Landscape

Project Management	Product Delivery	Process Improvement
Focused on achieving a specific outcome within defined parameters (time, cost, quality).	*Focused on successfully developing a specific deliverable or 'product'.*	*Focused on improving specific ways of working, to improve consistency, quality, and efficiency.*
PRINCE2 **P**rojects **In C**ontrolled **E**nvironments – A methodology to deliver projects based on 7 Principles, Practices, and Processes. **PMP** **P**roject **M**anagement **P**rofessional – A qualification from the Project Management Institute (PMI). Robust entry requirements before examination can be taken. **ChPP** **Ch**artered **P**roject **P**rofessional – A professional qualification from the Association for Project Management (APM) demonstrating technical knowledge, professional practice, and ethical behaviour.	**Agile** A software development methodology aimed at being adaptive to changing environments. Founded on 4 key values and defined by 12 principles. Centred around delivering smaller, more frequent items of value, and working in close teams with regular communication. **Scrum** A framework for delivering complex products in a manageable way. It establishes team roles (product owners, developers), methods (sizing, sprints), as well as tools (backlogs, daily scrums, etc.). **Waterfall** A cascading model of delivery where activities from one phase depend on the delivery of the previous phase being completed. A classic example being a 'requirements' phase, followed by a 'design' phase, followed by a 'delivery' phase.	**Six Sigma** A method of process improvement specifically focused on improving the quality of a process output. It uses statistical analysis, tools and methodologies to reduce the number of defects produced by a process. **Lean** Intended to remove waste from processes without impacting the overall customer value. Categorises waste by type and defines waste as an action that doesn't add value or isn't required by regulation, such as transportation, motion, overproduction, defects.

Figure 3

It is important to note that categories can overlap. For example, a project can be governed under PRINCE2 and have individual deliverables within it managed using Agile. At the same time, a project deliverable could be established to run a series of initiatives improving the performance of various processes using a methodology such as Lean or Six Sigma.

A note about Change Management

I deliberately haven't included a discipline I would describe as Change Management within this section. Some consultancies offer Project Management under the umbrella of Change Management. While there is some overlap, I believe the two disciplines offer significant differences and are quite distinct. Change Management tends to refer less to the implementation of change and more to the theory of change. Rather than delivering things that will provide benefits in the long term, it addresses how you drive behaviour in the long term. And while there is some overlap in terms of the level of creativity, I believe the skills and behaviours required are different enough to keep them as two distinct fields of expertise. Whereas Change Management addresses behavioural science and economics, how to nudge people to change the way they act, Project Management addresses Operational Excellence and how to get people to do things well.

In Conclusion

Change doesn't need to be that complicated. Projects can be extremely challenging given their scale and ambition, but that doesn't mean the challenges themselves are new or unique. Tools and technology may have added a new dimension, but the challenges faced by projects such as the building of the Hoover Dam still have relevance for many of today's projects, even if the scale of the change isn't as great.

A Project Manager who understands the challenges, knows the tools at their disposal, and is well versed in how to apply them, will be well placed to propose a solid strategy for approaching projects and be able to present that strategy with confidence and conviction.

The Principles

Chapter 3

People Before Processes

If I had to choose one element within a project that can almost guarantee certain success, it would be the people. If you have great people in the project team, you are 99% of the way to a great result.

Of course, this doesn't just relate to Project Management. But in my experience, it is the single biggest factor that is not given enough emphasis when teaching Project Management. So much focus is placed on the process that the people delivering projects become an afterthought. A project is a temporary operation, and I believe that understanding how to run an operation effectively is such an important foundation to establish that it forms the basis for this entire book. It's a simple theory I call 'The Hierarchy of Operational Excellence', and it states:

"To achieve optimal operational performance, an organisation must implement three key components: People, THEN Processes, THEN Systems."

I call it a hierarchy because the benefit to the performance of each component is cumulative. That is, the benefits of each element are dependent on, and limited by, the effectiveness of the preceding component.

This isn't groundbreaking or revolutionary, but it is something that's not widely understood. Many organisations place emphasis on the importance of people, but this is usually from a well-being perspective rather than a performance perspective. To help understanding, it's important to be clear on how each component benefits operational performance. In ridiculously simple terms, what do people, processes, and systems do?

- **People**
  do the actual work in an organisation that produces value.
- **Processes**
  help the people in the organisation do the work in the same way to get consistent results.
- **Systems**
  help the people work through the processes, connect People and Process, and capture information for future learning

Note that I use the term systems rather than technology. This is a deliberate distinction. Too often, technology is seen as a solution for organisational problems without a conscious understanding of its intended use.

My premise is that technology can be used as both a tool and a system. However, a system doesn't require technology. To help illustrate the point, think of an electronic till (cash register) at a grocery store. For the cashier scanning the groceries it is being used as a tool to make their job easier. The barcode scanner saves the cashier time by automatically recognising each item and then calculating the total. If cash is used, the cashier can enter the amount given, and the change is calculated automatically.

What's more, many tills can be connected centrally as a system to support other processes. Items scanned are automatically registered against the inventory of current stock, in turn triggering the automatic ordering of replacement stock. Payments from multiple tills update finance systems to support accounting processes, and recognition of customers via loyalty codes provides intelligent analysis to support marketing and sales promotions. In this instance, the technology is being utilised as part of a system.

Returning to the chapter topic, let's look at People, Processes, and Systems individually and in more detail.

People

The single most important component for Operational Excellence, and therefore, first in the hierarchy. Simply put, if you have great people, you will get great results. But how do we define 'great people'?

In a nutshell:

- **The right number of people**
  to meet the required demand without compromising the quality of the work they do.
- **With the right skills**
  to perform the specific roles they have, to the quality expected.
- **In the right locations**
  to perform the role effectively without introducing unnecessary barriers that impact quality.

- **With the right behaviours**

  and soft skills needed not only to perform the role but also to be part of a cohesive team of people.
- **And the right motivation**

  to ensure they continue to want to not only do the job well over time but also to grow and improve.
- **Aligned to the same vision**

  and pulling in the same direction with a clear understanding of how their job relates to the ultimate objective.
- **Using the right tools**

  to ensure they are spending as little time as possible on unnecessary tasks and maximising the return on effort.

If you achieve this, if you have great people, and only this, you are likely to get great results. However, getting those results might be more painful than it needs to be, and less efficient. The simplest way to illustrate this is to think of starting your own small business, a wooden furniture manufacturer for example, selling chairs and tables to customers in a local area. The first step would be to hire one or two good carpenters who you know can do the job well – people whose work you trust and who you know can produce the goods you need to a great standard. At the start, sales go well, and so to meet demand, you need to find more carpenters to help make more furniture. But as you hire more people, you find it hard to source people with as much experience as those in your current team or who are as high-performing. You double the amount of people, but you find that your people are now, on average, not as high-performing as they were. The variance in performance grows as you increase the number of people. Individuals perform tasks in a wider variety of ways, and not all of them know how to perform tasks as well as the highest performers. This is where processes come in.

Processes

Processes are simply a series of steps that people perform to complete a specific task. Having well-defined processes helps achieve results because:

- **They achieve consistency**
  by ensuring that the people doing the same tasks perform the same steps, in the same order, and with the same objective, so the chances of obtaining the same results are increased.
- **They improve efficiency**
  by defining the steps required to achieve an outcome, which means you can remove steps that take time to perform and that won't add value to the overall outcome.
- **They make learning new tasks easier**
  by giving new people a defined set of steps to follow, helping them be effective more quickly so they need less help from your other people.

So, to revisit the furniture manufacturing example, you've started with your handful of people in a single workshop.

You've expanded your team but are seeing a variance in the quality of products produced across the team. To solve this, you've come to the conclusion that processes may help improve consistency of performance, so you work with your best carpenters to understand the steps they perform and detail that as a guide for the other carpenters to follow. While this doesn't mean they are as experienced as carpenters overall, it does mean that for the specific products they are building, they are doing the things that are important to getting a good outcome as well as avoiding the things that result in a bad outcome.

As the business grows, you may decide to expand the business into another location. This will involve hiring new people in the new location where the skills you require may not exist or may not be as strong as in your original location. The guides you created can then be used to help new users accelerate their learning, and if they are followed consistently, this should eventually produce stable results.

However, what processes can't replicate or replace are the soft skills and behaviours that the top performers have. They can help ensure they are performing the steps that are deemed essential to a good outcome. They can help ensure people aren't performing steps that are unnecessary and wasting time. But they can't replicate the nuances of how to empathise naturally with customers or teach someone to think critically. If some of your carpenters are also tasked with taking customer orders, you may find that some are better at customer service than others. They may just be naturally more talkative, more extroverted. While your guides can help your team make products more consistently, they can't turn an introvert into an extrovert or motivate people who lack motivation. Put simply:

"You can't solve a People problem with a Process."

Another challenge with processes is that people don't necessarily have to follow them if they're just in a document. And this is where systems can help.

Systems

Systems are the icing on the cake, the amplification layer that acts as a multiplier of everything you've established by having the People and Process components in place. Systems perform the following functions:

- **They help People adhere to Processes**
  by building the processes into system interfaces so that users can be 'guided' through the steps automatically.
- **They connect People and Processes**
  by building multiple processes into a system so that people within different departments and locations can easily collaborate across a wider set of tasks.
- **They help organisations learn**
  by capturing data while users are working through processes, providing an opportunity to measure, analyse, and learn for future improvement.

Back to our example of an expanding business. Systems become increasingly important when scaling a process across a growing number of people, especially across multiple locations. They allow multiple processes performed across those locations to be connected and automated.

Imagine your furniture business has grown so large that it now needs a dedicated team to manage customer orders. A centralised system can allow a team of people in a call centre to process telephone orders from customers, allowing your carpenters to focus on making products. As this process is completed on an order system, the order can automatically be sent to the product team so that they can create the furniture requested by the customer. Once completed, the product team can trigger a process to another team, in another location, to distribute the finished product.

The system can also capture information about the customer, the people processing the order, the item ordered, and the process itself. All of this can be analysed over multiple interactions to provide insight into future production, marketing, customers, and improving processes.

The cumulative benefit

While all three components – People, Processes, and Systems – are essential to Operational Excellence, the cumulative effect is important. If you have great people, you'll get great results. If you add great processes, you'll get great results more consistently, more efficiently, and over a wider group of people. If you add great systems, your processes will get greater adherence, your People and Processes will have far greater integration, and you'll have a greater depth of information to enable learning and improvement.

Conversely, failure to implement robust processes and supporting systems as an organisation grows will almost guarantee a drop in business performance. Individual performance variance will grow, processes across varying locations will fail to integrate smoothly, and efficiency will decrease.

In its simplest form, I like to think of it as follows:

- **People** produce performance and results
- **Processes** improve efficiency and consistency
- **Systems** connect and inform

In Conclusion

The reason for detailing this Hierarchy of Operational Excellence theory is simple. Project Management methodologies are processes. They are often supported by systems that allow organisations to centrally monitor and report on the multiple projects that are being delivered at any point in time. But they don't address the area that has the biggest impact: the people. Most importantly, the person within the project who has the greatest impact on its outcome: the Project Manager.

So, while the focus has been driven predominantly by Project Management processes, this has removed the focus on what I believe is the most important factor in successfully delivering a project: the Project Manager. The Project Management Mindset aims to ensure that the cumulative benefit of People, Processes, and Systems can be fully realised by addressing the people element first.

Chapter 4

The Three Roles of the Project Manager

The central premise of The Project Management Mindset is that new Project Managers are being taught how to manage projects but not how to be Project Managers. They are learning the steps required to take a project from inception through to closure via the study of a Project Management methodology. And this cycle is somewhat self-perpetuating. The more we focus on teaching the process, the more important the process becomes.

If we want to focus on providing Project Managers with the skills and behaviours they need to succeed, we need to start by changing the way we think about the Project Manager role. At the centre of this change is the understanding that a Project Manager isn't just one role, it's three. Three distinct skill sets and behaviours that allow you to not only navigate the process of Project Management but to also add significant value. Skills that process steps can't teach, like how to lead a team or communicate challenging messages to senior leaders. Consulting with a client to help them expand a concept into an easily consumable proposal. The ability to stay focused on what matters when being pressured by competing priorities.

So, what are these three roles that require distinct skills and behaviours throughout the project? They are:

- **The Consultant**
- **The Planner**
- **The Leader**

Let's look at each role in detail, including what they do and what skills and behaviours are required to perform the role well.

Role Number 1: The Consultant
Overview

In my experience, the first role of a Project Manager is the least valued. Those who can perform it well establish projects with stronger foundations and inspire greater confidence in their ability to manage complex projects.

The start of any project begins with an idea. A small kernel of a project. A tiny snowball that, if robust enough, stays intact despite any bumps it encounters, and if significant enough, carries enough momentum to keep it moving through challenging terrain. A Consultant's role is to take this kernel of an idea and work with the Customer who originated it to prove that robustness and momentum. This is done through a series of increasingly intensive rounds of questioning, challenge, and documentation to help convince the Customer, and anyone else who needs to be convinced to invest time, money, or resources for the project to progress further.

The tasks of the Consultant

The Consultant has four simple but critical tasks to perform:

1. To understand, document, and challenge the Customer's requirements to ensure they can withstand rigorous scrutiny.

2. To assess the Customer's willingness and ability to proceed.

3. To create a strategy and plan to deliver the project's outcomes, manage its risks, and maintain oversight.

4. To plan, package, and present the proposal for a decision to proceed.

The required skills

To perform the role well, a unique set of competencies and behaviours is required.

The table below highlights each competency, along with situations in which they are utilised during the project.

Competency	Description	Required when?
Conceptual Interpretation	The ability to listen to an abstract concept, translate it into a solidified idea, and play it back to the intended audience in a clear, relatable, easy-to-understand manner.	Working with the Customer to understand requirements Working with challenges to the proposals Managing issues and concerns throughout the project

Commercial Awareness	Knowledge of business operations, awareness of the industry and operating environment, and the ability to overlay both to suggest opportunities or highlight potential challenges.	Working with the Customer to understand requirements Working with decision-makers to review the proposal
Narrative Presentation	The ability to prepare and present project updates simply and in a way that inspires confidence.	Presenting requirements to decision groups Providing progress updates throughout the project
Communication	Written and verbal communication with various individuals and groups to establish free-flowing information channels within the project.	Continuously throughout the project
Relationship Building	The ability to proactively build and nurture relationships.	Proactively and continuously throughout the project

While these competencies take time to develop and will require experience to perfect, the mindset tips throughout this book will help accelerate their comprehension. Individual coaching and mentoring can also help accelerate their development.

Role Number 2: The Planner
Overview
The second and probably most recognisable role is that of the Planner. While performing this role, the Project Manager plans and documents requirements to execute the project. These include the resources required as well as the budget. The Planner proposes an organisational structure for executing and overseeing the project. They also propose detailed deliverables linked to expected outcomes and ways to measure those outcomes. Additionally, the Project Manager develops a detailed project plan that is ready for execution, while utilising planning and modelling skills to prepare a digestible output to allow budget and resource requests to be reviewed. Task management skills are used to develop a step-by-step project plan to determine what needs to be done, by whom, when, and in what sequence. And finally, strong organisational skills are employed to ensure actions and questions are managed and responded to.

The tasks of the Planner:

1. To compile and maintain a detailed list of project deliverables, quality checks, and measures.

2. To create and maintain a detailed project plan, including risk management and quality assurance.

3. To create and maintain a reporting suite to track and monitor project progress.

4. To track actions, issues, and risks and facilitate resolution throughout the project.

The required skills

For this role, the skills and behaviours are more straightforward.

Competency	Description	Required when?
Project Planning	The ability to create a task-level plan linking outcomes to deliverables and tasks. Including assigning to individual users, time tracking, and linking dependent tasks.	When preparing initial plan for approval When updating the plan during Execution When preparing for the next sub-stage

Facilitation	The ability to bring a team of experts together to review requirements and plan tasks to deliver those requirements.	When preparing initial plan for approval When updating the plan during Execution When preparing for the next sub-stage
Task Management	The ability to create, assign, and track multiple tasks with multiple users in multiple locations.	When executing the project plan When managing ad-hoc issues and actions
Data Management and Reporting	Gathering and interpreting measures and metric data produced to report and update on project progress.	Continuously throughout the project

Role Number 3: The Leader

Overview

The Leader role is focused on leading the project team to execute the agreed project plan. It utilises team leadership skills to maintain momentum, energy, and motivation within the team. It manages day-to-day issues and challenges arising from the team and tasks, as well as requests from outside the project. While performing this role, a Project Manager seeks to maintain optimal performance from the project team, managing external pressures related to the project, while managing challenges from within the project team with the support of the Customer and Oversight Group.

The tasks of the Leader

1. To lead the project team through the Execution stage (and sub-stages) of the project.

2. To triage external requests and demands on the project on behalf of the project team.

3. To maintain the optimal performance and well-being of individual project team members.

4. To triage and escalate issues from within the project team that require external support.

The required skills

Compared to the previous two roles, the role of the Leader is far more soft-skill based, and many of the competencies are difficult to define. To help you with this, there is a chapter dedicated to the mindset of leadership later in the book.

Competency	Description	Required when?
Performance Management	The ability to manage individuals within a team to ensure peak performance,	Continuously throughout the project

	personal growth, and career development.	
Leadership Skills	The ability to motivate, energise, and challenge a team. To act as a figurehead. To build trust in the team to follow your vision.	When preparing initial plan for approval When updating the plan during execution When preparing for the next sub-stage
Communication Skills	The ability to communicate with the project team in a way that inspires confidence, trust, and honesty within the group.	When executing the project plan When managing ad-hoc issues and actions

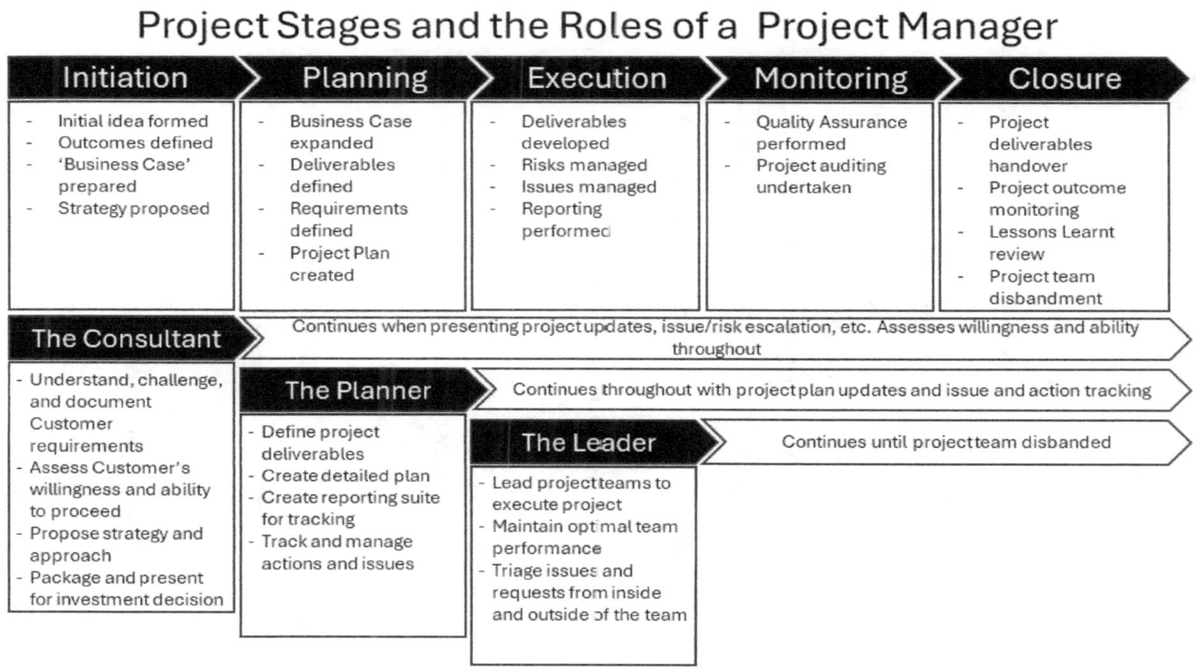

Project Stages and the Roles of a Project Manager

Initiation	Planning	Execution	Monitoring	Closure
- Initial idea formed - Outcomes defined - 'Business Case' prepared - Strategy proposed	- Business Case expanded - Deliverables defined - Requirements defined - Project Plan created	- Deliverables developed - Risks managed - Issues managed - Reporting performed	- Quality Assurance performed - Project auditing undertaken	- Project deliverables handover - Project outcome monitoring - Lessons Learnt review - Project team disbandment

The Consultant — Continues when presenting project updates, issue/risk escalation, etc. Assesses willingness and ability throughout

- Understand, challenge, and document Customer requirements
- Assess Customer's willingness and ability to proceed
- Propose strategy and approach
- Package and present for investment decision

The Planner — Continues throughout with project plan updates and issue and action tracking

- Define project deliverables
- Create detailed plan
- Create reporting suite for tracking
- Track and manage actions and issues

The Leader — Continues until project team disbanded

- Lead project teams to execute project
- Maintain optimal team performance
- Triage issues and requests from inside and outside of the team

Figure 4

While these roles generally align with the associated project stages, there is overlap. And the requirement for these roles and associated behaviours continues throughout the project. For example, the Consultant role is utilised through the Planning and Execution stages and when presenting to senior leaders for oversight. The behaviours required to summarise the project status and related updates in a manner that inspires confidence sit within that Consultant role. Similarly, the Planning role and its associated skills and behaviours are required continuously to respond to on-the-fly changes to ensure plans and other documents are updated and adjusted.

Understanding this concept allows a Project Manager to consciously choose which hat to wear at any point during a project. And wearing the right hat will increase your chances of executing the task at hand with confidence and skill.

In Conclusion

In my experience, most Customers think they need only a Planner. Subsequently, many Project Managers believe that being a Project Manager is being a good planner, and I understand why. On the surface, Project Management is about creating plans and managing tasks, issues, and risks. But the Consultant role is critical in setting up the project on solid foundations, and being a great Leader will mean the Execution stage is much more productive and less painful.

Many can perform one of the three roles well. Some can do two. But I've met very few who can perform all three well; Those who can have left a significant impression.

The Mindset Tips
The Consultant

Chapter 5

Know Your Customer and Why They Hired You

The reason for using a Project Manager is simple. Project Managers increase the probability that projects deliver the required outcomes on time, within budget, and to the right quality. They do this using a range of skills and behaviours alongside a process and set of tools to help them and the project team.

That alone sounds fine and provides a good description of the role. But we can go deeper than this to clarify the mindset of a great Project Manager. And to do this we need to understand why Project Managers are hired. While the answer might seem like an obvious "to increase the probability of a project delivering the required outcomes" and so on, I think we can make it simpler than that.

Customers hire Project Managers for two reasons:

1. **They don't have the time to manage the project themselves**
2. **They can't manage the project themselves**

But before we look into those two points in more detail, you'll note I refer to the 'Customer' throughout this book. Most methodologies will refer to a 'Sponsor' or 'Exec', but this is an unnecessary use of jargon that only adds confusion to a project. A Project Manager is there to help a Customer deliver an outcome. The Customer is paying the bills and calling the shots. They may need others to help call those shots and pay those bills, but they still make the ultimate decision. It doesn't mean they are always right, but they are the person you need to convince that you are the best person for the job throughout the project. Knowing who your Customer is and building a strong working relationship with that person is critical to being a successful Project Manager.

Now let's explore the two reasons for hiring a Project Manager in detail.

Reason 1: They don't have the time

A Customer might choose to hire a Project Manager simply because they are too busy to dedicate time themselves. Project Management requires a significant amount of time and effort to manage the administration, as well as the people. It requires mental dedication throughout the project to foresee and manage potential issues and opportunities.

A Customer may not have the will or the ability to dedicate this time and effort for that period. They may have the financial means to delegate this work and so avoid the effort. Or maybe dedicating their time and effort to a project will provide them with a better return than the cost of hiring a Project Manager. But without the time to do it themselves, there really is no option but to outsource if the project needs to go ahead.

Reason 2: They can't manage the project

The alternative is that the Customer may not have the ability to perform the role of a Project Manager. Project Managers bring multiple benefits, such as:

- **Experience**

  They know how to ask the right questions at the start of the project to ensure the original brief is developed into a workable plan. Having delivered similar projects multiple times, they are more likely to identify issues that commonly pose a risk to delivery.

- **Competency**

  They have the skills, tools, and behaviours to meet the challenges posed during project delivery.

- **Connections**

  They are likely to have a well-developed network of experts with a proven delivery record who can work on the project.

Understanding why your Customer hired you can help you proactively manage the most important relationship in your project. Misunderstandings can become painful for both parties, and in severe circumstances, they are potentially fatal (in project terms). Clarifying roles and responsibilities, mandates, communication methods, and boundaries will help flush out potential relationship-ending issues before they can begin.

To explore this further, let's look at some examples of situations in which a Project Manager might be hired.

1. **The Customer knows how to manage projects but doesn't have the time**

Managed positively, with clear boundaries and expectations, this can work very well. Having a Customer who knows what to expect, knows what a Project Manager needs to be supported, and can challenge effectively and supportively can be a positive experience. However, managed poorly, this risks working with a Customer who knows what they want, how they want it delivered, and simply wants someone to execute it on their behalf.

2. **The Customer knows how to manage projects and has the time**

In this scenario, the immediate question to explore is why the Customer isn't managing the project themselves. The reasonable answer, I think, lies within the definition of 'has the time'. Presumably the Customer has the funds to employ a Project Manager and has something more valuable they would rather spend their time on.

The clear risk here is that of an overly active Customer who wants to be more involved than they need to be. In this case, a robust agreement should be made between the Project Manager and the Customer, as in the first scenario, to agree what the 'how' looks like. Setting clear boundaries is essential, and positively enforcing these boundaries is crucial for relationship success. This could be captured in a Project Charter, or Terms of Engagement as I prefer to think of it, that details how the project will be run. This can be used as a reference during the project if issues arise.

3. The Customer doesn't know how to manage projects but has the time

This carries the same risk of an active Customer as the second scenario, and the solutions are the same, particularly when it comes to how updates should be provided. The secondary risk in this situation is that you are brought in to rescue an existing project that the Customer has tried but failed to manage on their own. If that is the case, the Project Manager could be taking on more than they bargained for and be walking into a challenging relationship from the start. In this case, I would be reluctant to adopt the project before undertaking a thorough review.

4. The Customer doesn't know how to manage projects and doesn't have the time

The most obvious and possibly ideal scenario in which to hire a Project Manager. The big risk here is that in the absence of knowledge, combined with an absence of time, the Customer may get nervous during the project from being unsure of the process. This may cause unnecessary disruption and effort for the Project Manager and the project team, and this could and should be avoided. In this situation, the Customer would likely benefit significantly from additional support and education on what to expect before the project starts. The Customer will want to know what is needed (and not needed) from them.

But there is another angle to consider. The Customer's perception of their capability and time. For example:

5. The Customer thinks they know how to manage projects and may or may not have the time

This can be particularly problematic. I've experienced numerous situations where a Customer knows what they want, how they want it, wants someone to execute on their behalf, but really doesn't know the fundamentals of Project Management. This situation poses the biggest challenge to a Project Manager. I'd go as far as saying you may seriously want to consider not undertaking a project in this situation. If you don't have a choice, or you feel you want to proceed, then the importance of discussing how you and the Customer see the relationship working is even greater than ever.

If full Project Management isn't required, then an upfront agreement of what is required can make this situation workable. For example, many Customers want project coordination. Someone to draft a plan and hold a pre-defined team to account for activity while reporting progress to an Oversight Group. While not ideal, it can work. However, I'd argue that the benefit for the Project Manager is minimal, although the need for long-term career progression needs to be weighed against that. A significant number of full-time employee Project Manager roles I have seen would fit into this category.

In Conclusion

The key theme running through these scenarios is the importance of a clear agreement between the Project Manager and the Customer about their working relationship and how they will interact throughout. Understanding a Customer's expectations of a Project Manager can be as important as understanding the outcomes they are attempting to achieve. Many believe they need a Project Manager, but few understand the full capability of the role or how it should be utilised to maximise the benefits.

Establishing this relationship properly at the beginning of a project will ensure you build solid foundations for success.

Chapter 6

Projects Don't Fail, Project Managers Do

The term 'project success' is commonly used to describe a project that meets its overall objectives within time, cost, and quality parameters. But there's another way to define project success – a way that helps Project Managers truly understand how to perform the Consultant role well and establish strong foundations for their project.

I like to look at it this way. Project success can be broken down into two categories:

- **Project success**
  Did the project achieve what it set out to achieve?
- **Project Management success**
  Was the project delivered within its original parameters (time, cost, budget)?

But even within that, there is some subjectivity and wiggle room that can add confusion. For example, when considering project success, does a project fail if it was experimental in nature? The building of a prototype to test an unknown outcome? A technology platform to test Customer adoption? A prototype vehicle to test Customer sentiment? If those tests are negative, does that mean project success or project failure?

More importantly when it comes to Project Management success, what if the parameters change during the project and the changes have been agreed by the Customer? What if the time or cost are impacted by factors unforeseen or completely out of the project's control? Should success be judged by whether or not those factors were foreseen as risks from the outset?

In the project success example, the key lies in the performance of the Consultant role. Defining what success looks like is key to being able to assess whether the outcomes were achieved. So in the case of an experimental project, where neither true nor false outcomes are wrong, then the success factor can be defined as proving or disproving a hypothesis.

In the 'Project Management' example, the answer is more nuanced. Project Management success does imply that the project is delivered within its original parameters, but I would add a caveat here: Was the project delivered within its original parameters (time, cost, budget) *unless otherwise agreed with the Customer and to their satisfaction?*

What I'm attempting to highlight here is that a binary, black-and-white definition of project success isn't as important as doing a great job for your Customer. Think of it this way. Overall project success is somewhat out of your control. As a Consultant, you can critique it, build the business case to support the hypothesis, and make sure it's thoroughly reviewed with the appropriate facts. But once the decision has been made to proceed, the only influence you have on the success of the project is to deliver it against the strategy and plan.

Project Management success, however, is firmly within your control. The time, cost, and budget are all factors that you define for the Customer to approve. Contingency within those variables should be proposed to allow some 'fat' in the plan, and potential risks to the project delivery should be identified and quantified, with mitigation plans defined to manage them. Assuming you've done that well and can execute well, you have done as much as you can to enable successful management of the project.

Remember, a Project Manager aims to increase the probability of Project Management success. But Project Management success doesn't guarantee the intended outcomes will materialise. That responsibility – and risk – lies with the Customer.

An alternative view of success

Another way of thinking about project success is looking at the reason projects fail. And by fail, I mean fail to execute. Usually this means being abandoned before completion and in a way that the Customer views as failure. Many projects are (and more should be in my opinion) shut down deliberately and positively because the case for change is no longer valid. In these circumstances, the closing of the project should not be seen as a failure.

In simple terms, projects fail because the Customer no longer has the willingness or the ability to continue. Either of these can become true at any point during the project. The proverbial straw that breaks the camel's back may be more specific, but the fundamental reason remains the same. As Project Managers, it is our responsibility to robustly assess the fundamentals of a project that influence those reasons for failure.

While this may seem over-simplistic, it helps a Project Manager frame how to perform the Consultant role well. Let's look at each of these reasons in isolation: the Customer's willingness to continue and their ability to continue.

The Customer's willingness to continue

Making changes of any kind involves some level of disruption and discomfort. Even decorating a room in your house requires a change to family routines while it's happening. Moving furniture, a level of mess, and some financial cost, for example. Even at this relatively small scale, many people delay starting the work because they're not prepared to go through the inconvenience. Scale this up to a bigger task and the change becomes a major challenge, and that unwillingness to endure disruption is even stronger. The shifting point for most tasks is when the need to undertake the activity outweighs the disruption or pain caused by undertaking it. More specifically, the perceived need to undertake the activity outweighs the disruption or pain. And that is a key point. As an experienced Consultant, your role is to help the Customer assess and quantify that perception, as well as the actual disruption and pain. A Customer may believe their perception is accurate, but your experience may help test the robustness of that perception.

This task alone has one of the biggest return-on-effort ratios of any single action you can undertake. Uncovering vulnerabilities in a Customer's willingness to proceed early in the project brings significant benefits: cost savings, time savings, and importantly, opportunity cost savings (it is far better to be spending time on something that is needed rather than wanted). And tackling this early on in the project can seriously bolster a Project Manager's credibility.

The Customer's ability to continue
The ability to continue relates more to the variables outside the Customer's control. Even if it has been established that the Customer is willing to proceed and accepts the anticipated level of disruption, there may be other variables that can't be solved. The obvious example is finances. The money required to make the desired change may not be available, or a decision may have been made to spend it elsewhere. The resources may not be available (people or equipment) at the time they are needed. What's more, the decision to proceed may be out of the Customer's hands alone. Decisions about money, resources, the law, who makes those decisions, may mean the inability to continue prevents the project from moving forward.

Again, the role of a Consultant is to assess and attempt to quantify the ability to continue and robustly challenge the project's continuation. Similar to a peer review of academic publications, a good-faith, healthy challenge of the project's long-term viability performed in the early stages of a project acts as a fantastic safety net for the Customer and the project team.

And finally, it is worth noting that while a Customer's willingness and ability may be distinct from each other, they are linked. For example, the perceived disruption and pain of the project (and therefore the willingness) can be increased by the actual execution of the project. Put another way, a poorly run, inefficient project may be more painful and disruptive than was expected or planned for, therefore diminishing the willingness to continue. Similarly, a misunderstanding of the overall outcomes may alter the willingness of key influencers mid-project.

A simple assessment

So how do we go about assessing the willingness and ability to proceed? It's conceptually quite simple. A series of consultation sessions with the Customer and others involved to iteratively review, discuss, and document the following points will quickly build a picture of the project fundamentals:

- **What are we proposing to do?**
  A really simple, plain-worded description of what the proposal is. For example: "We want to move our office and all our people from location X to location Y."
- **What problem are we trying to solve?**
  This is the 'why' for the project. Some don't like problem statements as they see them as negative (see Chapter 9). The idea of getting to the bottom of this is to allow the exploring of alternative options. Too often have I seen alternatives raised deep into project execution when a project is facing difficulties.

- **What happens if we don't do it?**

  To support the challenges from the question above and significantly help with prioritisation, I recommend answering in the negative. For example: "We increase the risk of losing key customers to competitors, leading to decreased revenue and market share."

- **What outcomes do we expect to achieve?**

  If we intend to undertake a project that will likely take significant effort, money, and time, it's important to be clear on what we expect to achieve from it. While these expectations don't need to be fully detailed at the first-drafting stage, it is important to make them clear and tangible. For example:

  - Reduced operational expenditure
  - Increased customer satisfaction
  - Increased key customer retention rate

- **How would we know if we had achieved them?**

  This is where we try to be more specific about our outcomes. Again, they don't need to be final, but they should be a realistic estimation and provide a form of measurement. Such as:

  - Operational expenditure reduced by £X from £Y to £Z
  - Customer satisfaction score for key clients up from X to Y
  - Customer retention rates increased from X to Y (or possibly maintained if there is expectation that they drop)

- **Why does it need to be done now?**

  This simple question serves two key purposes. In its minimal form, it helps prioritise the project against a portfolio of other projects. Secondly, and this is where a Consultant can add value again, it helps challenge the Customer on whether the project really needs to be done now, a challenge that is likely to be raised by others.

- **Why should it be done instead of other projects being proposed?**

  This question may not be possible to answer at the initial stage, depending on knowledge of what else is being proposed that may compete with your project. The challenge with this question is ensuring your project is prioritised fairly while also ensuring any comparison against competing projects is fair and credible. I would recommend basing the response around a belief or compelling argument. For example: "We believe the reputational threat of losing key customers poses more of a business risk than failing to launch a new product."

- **How much would it cost (approximately)?**

  At this stage, cost assumptions will be high-level estimates, mainly for comparison to the potential outcome measurements for a return on investment decision and prioritisation against other projects. The important things to indicate at an early stage are:
  - How much the project is estimated to cost in total

- What the potential variance could be
- What amount of that cost is existing (for example, staff already employed)?
- What amount of that cost would be new (for example, new staff/equipment)?
- Over what period the spend would be expected

- **How long do we expect it to take?**

As with the budget, this should be high-level, indicating approximate timelines for completion. At this point, timelines can be indicated for key stages or 'milestones' to help give some context. For example, project planning between (months and year), execution between (months and year), project closure and monitoring between (months and year). Timelines should be loose enough to allow for contingency (preferably by considering previous experience) without risking credibility. The key to maintaining credibility is to ensure you can talk through your timelines and contingency with clear reasoning for why you believe it's required.

- **What would we need to do it?**

This should be a high-level view of what would need to be in place to execute the project. It should cover items like people (which roles, teams, etc.), equipment (offices, hardware, tools, etc.), and technology (software, comms, etc.). This should be as detailed as possible, albeit that more detail may come to light with detailed further planning.

- **What could go wrong during the project?**
This should be a simple list of negative consequences that could be introduced by attempting the project, as well as events that could mean the need to terminate the project before completion. This allows for potential consequences/events to be challenged at an early stage, as well as factoring them into plans so that they can be managed. For example:
- By moving office, we may disrupt out customer service and make it worse
- By moving office, we may lose some of our key team members
- Real estate costs could fluctuate mid-project, impacting our costs significantly
- **Would anyone object to it being done?**
While this is a subjective view, a key challenge to identify early within the project is whether there are any individuals or groups who would be opposed to the proposed outcomes, and if so, to then assess how influential their objections could be. While this could be captured in the 'What could go wrong' section above, the subject is important enough to warrant a separate section, in conjunction with a separate set of activities planned to manage the challenges.
- **How would we plan to approach it?**
The final part to address is the strategic approach. By this I mean how we plan to tackle each of the above points. In order to make progress through to planning, it's useful to indicate what you plan to do to progress

and why, effectively telling the 'story' of the approach. This story should document answers to each of the questions above, while also proposing next steps to address the expected challenges. For example, if a decision maker is unconvinced that the financial benefit is there, it may be worth indicating that an early approach is to perform a financial analysis to confirm assumptions. Market research or staff surveys may be proposed early in the project to address any concerns about the loss of staff as a result of moving location.

In scope/out of scope
Note, I don't reference 'scope'. This is intentional. It's an area where I differ from many within the industry. While many see the definition of scope as marking the project's boundaries, I see it as unnecessary jargon that adds very little value. It can also result in ambiguity and confusion between the Customer and the Project Manager. If pushed, I can see an argument for detailing what is out of scope, purely for the purpose of taking any potential ideas off the table that the Customer is absolutely against at the outset. But the specific deliverables established during the Planning stage *explicitly* declare what is to be delivered to achieve the outcomes.

In Conclusion
The questions in this chapter form the basis of the case for change, the narrative of the project. More work is required beyond this point to collate and document the information,

and more work may be required to challenge some of the assumptions. For example, the estimated cost of the project may require deeper investigation and modelling. Understanding who may object to the proposals and what risks may be present may require further research. However, through the process of answering these questions, we build a thorough picture of a Customer's willingness and ability to proceed. Individual methodologies will have standard tools, documents, and processes for capturing this information. This chapter simply highlights what is important for a Project Manager to understand while performing the Consultant role.

Chapter 7

Maintain a Self-Employed Mindset

I've long held the belief that Project Management is a profession best performed as a self-employed contractor because it presents numerous benefits. It allows a Project Manager to remain independent from the day-to-day workings of an organisation and focus solely on the project. It provides the benefit of exposing an individual to a wider range of businesses and projects, effectively making them a stronger Consultant. And lastly, potentially most importantly, it prevents the Project Manager from being a direct employee of the Customer, removing any conflicts of interest within the single most important relationship within a project.

However, most Project Managers will be hired as a permanent employee, and while the job and income security are an obvious positive, full-time employment introduces an insidious challenge for Project Managers. Being self-employed may not be an option for most, but maintaining the mindset of a self-employed contractor can help ensure you approach the project, issues, and relationships in a sustainable way.

One potential issue for permanently-employed Project Managers is feeling compelled to take personal ownership of the project's outcomes. And as we've already covered, it's a commonly held opinion that a Project Manager's job is to deliver the desired outcomes on time, within budget, and to the desired quality. At first glance this seems reasonable, but it can lead to a problematic perception of the role. Project Managers are actually there to help increase the probability of the outcomes being delivered on time, to budget, and to the desired quality.

While the difference is subtle and the latter may seem a little non-committal, that difference is significant. Project Managers increase the probability of success, but they don't guarantee success. A Project Manager is hired because they have the expertise and experience to deliver a complex set of deliverables where the Customer doesn't. Put simply, the project will run more smoothly with them involved than it will without them.

The challenge occurs when a Customer has an unrealistic expectation that the outcomes are guaranteed. As an independent contractor without an employer/employee dynamic, that conversation can be challenged during the initial discussions. For full-time employees, the Customer may be a direct line manager or someone senior in the organisation with a direct influence over the Project Manager's career. In this case, challenging the Customer (and line-manager) can be more difficult and may impact both the project and long-term prospects of the Project Manager.

Even more challenging is being assigned to projects that are doomed to fail from the outset – projects that have not been through a robust consultation and healthy challenge. And in what are often described as 'Nike projects' (just do it!), a Project Manager's ability to succeed may be limited by the competency of the project's early stages.

In these situations, the mindset of a Project Manager is key. While you may not be an independent consultant, thinking of yourself as one can help you approach these situations correctly. Done poorly, or not at all, you might find yourself pushed into trying to own and solve the projects and issues, leading to a painful project experience and a potential loss of credibility as a reward for your efforts. Done correctly, a healthy, positively-pitched challenge can establish what is effectively a self-employed status – and confirmation that the Project Manager is a value-adding consultant.

To help establish this self-employed mindset, let's look at some specific instances where it could be useful. The following three scenarios are situations I've experienced during my career, in order of how often I've encountered them, together with how each one can be managed effectively.

Scenario 1 – Late-stage Project Manager engagement

Description:
In this scenario a project is already through the concept stage, and a Project Manager is assigned to help coordinate the execution of the project.

Potential Issues:
In these situations, which are unfortunately extremely common, the key assessment stage has passed, meaning the Consultant role cannot be performed. Without this, a Project Manager risks accepting accountability for executing a project that might be fundamentally flawed. It also means the Project Manager has not had the benefit of building the narrative and strategy, and so is not fully engaged or bought into the project.

Project resourcing may have already been defined and put in place, giving the Project Manager very little influence over the critical set-up of the project.

Recommended approach:

The key element here is early positive challenge. As a Project Manager, the goal is to not accept any projects that are likely to be unsuccessful. Your long-term reputation is based on the continuous successful management of projects. As a self-employed Project Manager, the reputational cost of taking on a flawed project would likely outweigh any benefit received. But as a full-time employee, the choice may be out of your control. In this instance, for the benefit of both you and the project, it is essential that you assert the need for proper due diligence. Doing this before proceeding allows you to raise concerns – even if you are being instructed to proceed. When I've done this in the past, I've used the benefit of 'being the idiot in the room' (see *Chapter 11*). Doing this alongside my skills as a Consultant means I can insist on asking the questions that are needed to help frame the project correctly. Customers may understandably want to resist revisiting the fundamentals; they are likely to be trying to accelerate delivery. But explaining the benefits of a short-term review vs. the long-term benefit of avoiding unnecessary pain is usually effective. Use phrases such as "I'm concerned about the risk this project poses" or "If I were an independent contractor, I'd be concerned about …"

Scenario 2 – Allocation of multiple projects

Description:

In this scenario, a Project Manager is expected to manage multiple projects at the same time, sometimes at varying stages of the project life cycle.

Potential Issues:

Again, an extremely common situation and one that as a self-employed Project Manager is ultimately within your control. Having individual external clients allows a selective approach to taking on new work. That isn't to say you may not choose to overlap, but you have the control over when and how you do it. The Customer may have the option of delaying the start of a project to accommodate your schedule. They may assume that you are at capacity and would be unable to support their work effectively if you started immediately. But as a full-time employee, it is more likely that a judgement has already been made about your capacity. Any resistance on your part may be seen as a reluctance to contribute or as you not being a team player.

Recommended Approach:

This scenario is likely to indicate that the role of a Project Manager is being under-appreciated. In my experience, the assignment of multiple projects is often due to the need for someone to help coordinate a series of tasks for a team and bring some structure to the delivery rather than the need for full Project Management. As with the previous scenario, positivity is essential. The key is to ensure the Customer understands the benefits of a Project Manager being able to spend the appropriate amount of time managing projects well and, more importantly, understands the risks of them not having the capacity to perform multiple projects well. While these can be difficult to articulate, similar arguments to Scenario 1 apply.

Additionally, detailing some of the lesser-understood time requirements can help with the discussion. Provide details of activities that are required regularly: project meetings, updating of project plans, daily team calls, Oversight Group updates, and so on. Creating a simple summary of the time required per week for each of these will help quantify overall time requirements. Once this is done and you have a view of minimum time requirements per week, you will be able to move on to more positive proposals.

A reasonable compromise solution for this is to request additional project support to help spread the load. Adding a Project Planner or Junior Project Manager to support the workload would be my recommendation. It gives the Project Manager more time to focus on the value-added activity. But another compelling benefit is the opportunity to build the long-term change capability of the organisation by developing the potential of future Project Managers.

Scenario 3 – Under-resourcing of projects

Description:

In this scenario, you have a well-defined resource plan but have not been granted the full resources required to meet that plan. Some roles are not filled at all, or they are filled, but with people who are also performing another role.

Potential Issues:

This is an extremely common situation to find yourself in as a Project Manager. Organisations often feel project resourcing can be done alongside normal activity, without the additional cost or disruption of seconding people out of their day jobs. This poses an immediate and obvious risk to the timelines of a project, and the impact of the resource gap can be more than the sum of its parts. The assumption that people spending 50% of their time on project work and 50% on their normal role will result in only a 50% delay is false. The handover between roles takes time. Even without that inefficiency, the impact of the extended timelines is greater than their total because they affect the sequencing of dependent tasks. This also tends to create a significant amount of additional work for the Project Manager in terms of coordination and tracking. And for the individuals concerned there is a difficult challenge here: how to balance their time between roles, particularly when immediate demands tend to take precedence.

Recommended Approach:

This is a difficult challenge to approach. The common root of this issue is often that a Customer or their organisation believes that requests for resources are submitted 'optimistically', a luxury, as it were. Wanting to run lean operations is a perfectly understandable ambition and is best done over time through process improvement activities. Projects, however, should be run on opportunities that present a sizable enough return to warrant robust investment. Proposals to resource projects lightly are best countered with a business case that shows a strong return on investment.

And there lies the key to managing this scenario. Focusing on a robust business case with a significant return on investment, combined with a thoroughly reviewed resource plan, should make the case for investment and resource simple. In the spirit of a self-employed contractor, positioning the question as "If the case for change is strong enough, why would we think about risking the outcome?" is a strong, positive way to push back. And if this approach is not successful, and you are unable to decline the project, my next recommendation would be to formally introduce resourcing as an execution risk to the project. Producing measures and metrics around the execution of the project and the availability of resources can help keep the conversation live and serve as early proof of your concerns (see *Chapter 11*). One final approach I recommend is formulating and presenting various alternative scenarios based on the potential risk, then asking the Customer to choose their preferred approach in light of the associated consequences. For example, producing low-, mid-, and high-risk scenarios along with the associated impacts on timelines is a good way to illustrate the issue.

In Conclusion

There's no escaping that these are difficult waters to navigate, and there isn't always a solution in the most difficult situations. But there are approaches that can help mitigate negative outcomes. And while the scenarios in this chapter are not exhaustive, they give a flavour of how to apply the self-employed mindset and take advantage of it, even if you are not in a position to be self-employed.

The Mindset Tips
The Planner

Chapter 8

Own Nothing, and Keep Your Customer Happy

The worst thing about being a Project Manager is that you don't actually produce any of the things that matter. The best thing about being a Project Manager is that you don't actually produce any of the things that matter!

Before I became a Project Manager, I was more of a technical specialist. My background was in database administration and web development. Oracle Databases, SQL, HTML, JavaScript and ASP, building data-driven websites back when data-driven websites were new and exciting. I loved the creativity. The simple concept of having a problem to solve and there being numerous ways to solve it. Mostly, I loved the ability to isolate myself for hours at a time and just produce work. No distractions, no fixed hours, just me and the work.

As my career progressed, I moved into more analytical roles. Data analysis, Excel VBA Macros, and the like. That progressed through to business analysis and process improvement, utilising my technical skills to bridge the gap between technical teams and business teams. I seemed to possess a somewhat rare ability to speak the language of both sides of my organisation. This role gave me the ability to utilise my technical skills and still enjoy indulging in the work while being able to solve larger, more important questions. Over time, this led me to Project Management and the opportunity to solve bigger problems and make larger changes.

But this shift wasn't an easy one. Until that point, I'd been building my skills and capabilities in a smooth, linear fashion. More responsibility, more exposure, more learning. However, the change to Project Management posed a tangential shift that I struggled to manage. I was a 'doer'. Someone who valued producing work as a solo contributor. Someone who based their reputation on the quality of their individual output. As a Project Manager, this would no longer work.

The challenge of being a Project Manager is that of owning nothing. Rather than being a contributor, producing an individual piece of a larger whole, the Project Manager moves to being responsible for and coordinating that larger whole. No longer the virtuoso performer in the orchestra, now the conductor. No longer focused on the individual notes for their specific instrument but focused on directing the entire symphony.

And when you find value and motivation in focusing on the individual task, on the mastery of a few specific skills, this transition can be difficult. The temptation may remain to perform the tasks you know you can do well yourself or pick up the slack when things are struggling. To lock yourself away and grind out some work to help the project along in the difficult times. But like a conductor focusing only on one section of the orchestra, the result will be an uncoordinated, dissonant mess, and an audience left unsatisfied by the resulting performance.

But if you can make the transition, you soon realise that owning nothing is a feature of the role rather than a bug. And rather than seeing it as a failure or a lack of production, you soon start to adopt a different mindset. The mindset of a true leader. The simple acceptance that your performance and your reputation aren't the sum of the work you produce yourself. Rather, your value is the sum of the volume and quality of the work produced by your team.

And herein lies the paradox. Within the challenge of being a Project Manager, the fact you own nothing is actually the opportunity. If you can master this essential mindset shift, you can leapfrog a significant amount of pain that many new Project Managers experience. But it's not easy. There will be pressure within projects. Expectations from your Customer or others in the organisation, as well as demands from within the project team that put immediate pressure on you. And if like me you pride yourself on getting things done, meeting deadlines, and responding to pressure, then you possibly risk winning the short-term battle at the cost of the long-term campaign. The wisdom in this comes from knowing that while your Customer, or your team, might feel like they are getting what they *want*, your role is actually to give them what they *need*.

Managing this takes tact, but if established correctly from the beginning, it can be quite simple. With prevention being better than any cure, I like to use the following techniques:

1. Clearly establish roles and responsibilities
At the start of a project, when planning and detailing the strategy, clearly set out the expectations of the Project Manager. An early education session with the Customer and

Oversight Group can go a long way in setting the tone for the remainder of the project.

2. Resource effectively

When establishing your project resource requirements, ensure there is capacity included for managing project demands. I've long been a fan of lobbying (usually unsuccessfully) for a Project Administrator or a Junior Project Manager within my project teams. As we discovered in the previous chapter, this type of role has two key benefits. Firstly, it provides the capacity and flexibility to perform a large amount of project coordination that silently benefits the overall project. It also has the benefit of developing the Junior Project Manager's career in the process.

3. Challenge resource gaps

The inability to respond to immediate requests may be indicative of a project team that isn't resourced correctly. Assuming (as per The Hierarchy of Operational Excellence in *Chapter 3*) that you believe your people have the right skills, motivation, and the like, then the challenge may be that you don't have enough people. Or at least you have the right number of people, but they don't have enough time. Early signs of the inability to respond to urgent issues should be used to question project resourcing as a basic health check.

Specialists vs. Generalists

There's another important angle to this that is worth addressing, something that has become more of an issue in the last few years as I have been writing this book: the rise of

'Specialist' Project Manager roles. In *Chapter 4*, we saw what Project Management was introduced to do, what problems it was introduced to solve, and what Project Managers do to help solve that problem: add control and discipline to complex, large-scale activities and attempt to deliver them within pre-defined parameters. Project Managers tend to have specific industry experience. This reduces the learning curve and makes it more likely they are able to critique the case for change and have experience and a network of experts they can turn to who understand the subject of the project.

But increasingly, particularly within technology, we are seeing a focus on recruiting super-specialised Project Managers. Project Managers who not only need to have experience within an industry but also have experience of specific disciplines within that industry. For example, an Information Technology Transformation Project Manager who must have pharmaceutical industry experience, along with experience delivering cloud-based solutions focused on cyber security.

These types of roles suggest either a serious misunderstanding of what a Project Manager should be or an evolution into the space of what I'd term 'Specialised Project Management'. While the latter might be the case, I'd suggest this falls firmly into the category of product delivery. Someone with technical experience and the ability to get 'hands on', who can also do some coordination of other people, along with some planning and reporting. A Customer asking for specific skills in a

Project Manager should be a red flag. It suggests the project is a *fait accompli*, a topic we covered in *Chapter 5*.

To be a Project Manager is to be a generalist. We don't own the solutions, and we don't own the delivery. We don't produce the things that get us to our outcome. We coordinate and facilitate other experts who can deliver those things. We provide expertise to ensure the initiative is viable. We drive the investment case and map out the roadmap for how we get from concept to outcome, and then plan it in detail. And finally, we lead the team in executing that plan.

Experience is useful but not essential. We work with business users who want to achieve an outcome, and we use our ability to manage through the unknown to achieve it. We manage the bigger picture. We work with experts who know the specific subject matter for individual components. We don't know the details to a technical level, and that is not a failing, it is by design.

In Conclusion

The thought of 'owning nothing' may seem like poor commitment on the surface, particularly if your background is similar to mine. But not taking ownership is not only beneficial to you, it is also essential for the success of the project's delivery. It allows you to coordinate and facilitate the ownership of numerous individual tasks, leading to a single, significant outcome, and it is critical for knowing how to be a great Project Manager.

Chapter 9

Create Problems, Deliver Solutions

Defining the specific things that need to be delivered to achieve the Customer's desired outcome is one of the key tasks performed in the role of the Planner. At first, this might seem like a trivial task, almost a given. However, where outcomes are known but deliverables are yet to be determined, this can be quite the task. And a key question to ask when defining the project's deliverables is:

"How do you know which things will actually achieve your outcomes?"

The short answer is you don't. The very nature of a project means attempting to achieve an outcome for a Customer in a manner that is as risk-free as possible. And as we know from previous chapters, there are three principles that can help us achieve this:

1. People provide the value

The first thing to remember is that it's the people who provide the value. The workstream leads in your project team are placed there because they are experts in their given area. They are best positioned to define what needs to be built, given the outcomes required. They may not have the answers themselves, but they have a series of Subject Matter Experts to call upon to help with the definition. Let your experts within the team define what the individual deliverables should be.

2. Own nothing

Once we've let our experts define the deliverables, we can rely on the principle of owning nothing. The delegated authority, staged approach is key. Remember that although your project workstream leads propose the deliverables, it's the Customer with the support of the Oversight Group who decide to accept or reject them. And while the workstream leads and their network of experts are likely to make the most informed recommendations, a strong Customer may require some convincing. A rationale should be provided to the Customer to help with that decision, and while the form that rationale takes can vary significantly, it should be as objective as possible. For example, if the recommendation is 'to improve the competency of the sales team', then you'd expect at least some analysis and modelling of the current and future state to be performed and presented: a small business case to explain why the deliverable should work, what the expected benefit should be, and how it can be measured.

3. Delivering in stages

The staged delivery approach also provides a mechanism that adds more certainty. If specific deliverables are critical, a 'test and learn' stage can be included in the Execution stage of the project. For example, for a project to develop a new vehicle in a competitive market, a period of market research would be wise, and it could be planned as an initial stage to provide some control around viability of the project. This provides a relatively low effort, minimal investment approach to minimise the risk in your plan.

And then, there's a fourth principle to consider.

4. Framing negatively

When it comes to documenting a convincing strategy that aligns deliverables to outcomes, I take a negative approach. That is to say, I like to phrase things in terms of problem statements. While some prefer a positive approach to outcomes or deliverables, I find people relate to problems more positively. They tend to be easier to word and easier to understand. I also find most people tend to prioritise solving problems over pursuing opportunities. Perhaps we are wired to tackle the things that will make our lives worse before we tackle the things that might make our lives better.

Take the following example.

> ### The Opportunity
> "Expanding our business into Western Europe could increase our gross revenue by 10% per year."
>
> ### As a Problem
> "We're losing 10% gross revenue per year by not being in Western Europe."

There is something slightly more compelling about the second statement. The language around problems tends to be more efficient, and there's an implicit urgency and potency, a call to action. But when using problem statements, be careful not to fall into the trap of exaggerating the problem. You may be tempted to word a statement along the lines of "Not being in Western Europe will cost us 10% of gross revenue and likely lead to the business failing", but the aim isn't to catastrophise, merely to frame things in the negative.

To map out specific deliverables, I try to answer the following questions:

- What outcome are we trying to achieve?
- What does that mean in more detail?
- What problems are preventing us from achieving the outcome?
- How do we aim to solve those problems?
- What specifically will we do to solve those problems?

Let's look at an example.

- **What outcome are we trying to achieve?**
  - We want to have the number one selling small car in the UK

- **What does that mean in more detail?**
  - We want to develop a new hybrid small family car that will sell more in the UK in the first two years after launch than any of its equivalent rivals

- **What problems are preventing us from achieving the outcome?**
  - We don't have a hybrid engine in our inventory
  - People don't associate our brand with small cars
  - We can't price competitively in the UK as we manufacture in other countries

-   **How do we aim to solve those problems?**
    - We need to develop a class-leading hybrid engine
    - We need to understand our target audience and develop a car to meet their needs
    - We need to build brand awareness within the small family vehicle market
    - We need to move manufacturing to the UK or significantly reduce production and shipping cost

-   **What specifically will we do to solve those problems?**

    Develop a leading hybrid engine
    - A new hybrid engine design
    - A hybrid engine prototype

    Understand our target audience and develop a car
    - Research and development of a new car

    Brand awareness for target market
    - Market research into the target market
    - Marketing and branding material and campaigns

Move manufacturing to the UK or significantly reduce production and shipping costs
- Financial modelling to determine site build vs. cost reduction
- A manufacturing site to build the car and engine

In Conclusion

In reality, building a view of deliverables linked to the outcomes is an iterative and intensive process. It may also develop throughout the project – some deliverables will not be known until other decisions have been made. For example, building a manufacturing site in the UK would not be a firm deliverable until the modelling and decision had been made to move manufacturing instead of pursuing cost reduction.

Outcomes, Problems, and Solutions

Desired Outcome

We want to have the number one selling small car in the UK

What does that mean in more detail?

We want to develop a new hybrid small family car that will sell more in the UK in the first two years after launch than any of its equivalent rivals.

What problems are stopping us?	How do we solve them?	What specifically?
We don't have a hybrid engine in our inventory that we can use	*We need to develop a class-leading hybrid engine*	- *A new hybrid engine design* - *A new hybrid engine prototype*
People don't associate our brand with small cars	*We need to understand our target audience and develop a car that meets their needs* *We need to build brand awareness within the small family vehicle market*	- *Research and Development of a new car* - *Market research into the target market* - *Marketing and branding material* - *Marketing campaigns*
We can't price competitively in the UK as we manufacture in other countries	*We need to move manufacturing to the UK, or significantly reduce the production and shipping costs*	- *Financial modelling to determine site build vs. cost reduction* - *A manufacturing site to build the car and engine (dependent on above)*

Figure 5

The Mindset Tips
The Leader

Chapter 10

The Confidence Game

To be a Project Manager, you need to be able to manage projects. To do it well, you need to inspire confidence.

In *Chapter 6*, we covered what Project and Project Management success looks like. But as we have seen, Project Manager success is slightly harder to define. In one sense, Project Manager success is somewhat of a circular reference. To be a successful Project Manager, you need to successfully manage projects! But as a new Project Manager, that's not very helpful. I think we can do a little better:

"A successful Project Manager successfully manages projects while maintaining the confidence of the Customer and the wider project team."

Managing projects is what we do well. Maintaining the perception of confidence is how we do it well.

If I could summarise the most positive perception a Customer could have of a Project Manager, it would be as a 'Trusted Advisor'. There is more to the role, of course, but gaining the Customer's trust is key.

Everyone involved will have moments of doubt and stress at various points in the project. Customers will want constant assurance that the project will deliver as expected. Individuals who are dependent on or have a vested interest in the project will seek the same. Project team members who are under significant pressure to deliver will seek protection from outside influences and require a steady ship during the inevitable choppy waters.

In providing assurance to others (and in line with the self-employed mindset of *Chapter 7*), I'm always conscious of the perception they have of me, of my personal brand. I want to deliver successful projects and provide great value as that will be what my services will be judged on. But more than this, I want to leave my Customer with no doubt in their mind that I am the person they can trust to run future projects.

Every interaction I have with any individual in the course of managing a project leaves an impression. And while not every interaction will be positive, I aim at the very least to instil confidence that I am capable within my role. I want to leave a positive 'net promotor score' so that my reputation leaves an echo in the organisation after the project has completed.

But this doesn't apply only to my Customers. I want everyone working on the project to have the same perception. And there are two reasons for this. Firstly, someone working in the project team today may be a project leader in the future and is therefore a potential Customer. Secondly, I don't want productivity to suffer because team members are being distracted by perceived concerns or issues.

So how do you inspire confidence within your projects? The simple answer is constantly! In reality it's conceptually simple, but it does require some discipline and the right mindset. I find the following helps.

Communicate Often

As a general rule, I try to establish the following routine within my projects

Weekly project team meetings

About an hour on a Monday morning with the core project team. Review progress against plan, outstanding and upcoming tasks, and support that anyone may need. Sets the tone for the week.

Daily scrums/stand-up meetings

A 15-minute informal session for those working on specific deliverables in the project. Purely to ensure engagement, keep momentum, and cast light on any potential issues the moment they happen.

Weekly project updates

A Friday summary that goes out to the same audience as the Monday morning project team meeting. Summarises the status of the plan and actions reviewed on the previous Monday, as well as a preview of what will be covered the following Monday.

Weekly governance updates

A very high-level update of the project that shows a simple view of the project's progress against agreed parameters. Contains an executive summary and key upcoming events or deliverables.

Monthly oversight reviews

Monthly seems about right for governance oversight, but the frequency is often set by the Customer and the organisation. Should be pitched at a high-to-medium level and in a regular format. I prefer to keep these sessions as a visual walk-through, with as little discussion as possible. The aim is to guide them through the project status in a controlled, structured fashion.

Communicate Honestly

While this might seem obvious, it's critically important and often missed. Being honest with both the Customer and the project team helps avoid speculation, but it can be a difficult balance. The line between being honest and not divulging information is a blurry one. If you know a project is being de-scoped or a team scaled down, do you tell the project team immediately? If you discover a serious issue in the project, do you tell the governance team right away? While there's no single right answer, my guiding principle is to ensure that when you share the information, you have taken the time to:

- Fully understand the issue and its implications and condense it down to what is purely factual.

- Discuss and challenge the issue with whoever highlighted it. Make sure, based on your understanding, that you've fully grasped the issue (see above) and are comfortable that you agree with it and its implications.

- Clarify your perspective on the issue. Ensure your personal views on it are clear and that you can articulate them in a sensible, calm manner and in good faith.

Communicate Simply and Be Human

This is arguably the most important aspect. The way you communicate will set the tone for how you are perceived. Keeping communications simple and in plain terms is essential. People will be looking to you to set the tone and decide whether they need to be concerned.

I've been a dog owner for many years and am hyper-aware that minute changes in my body language have a significant influence on how my dogs perceive things. If I am excitable, they become excitable. If I look nervous, they know to be nervous. I try to take the same approach when working on projects. In formal updates I write simply, without jargon, and punctuate frequently. I make verbal communication clear, concise, and deliberate. I think about body language. How I sit, whether I touch my face or hair a lot. I think about my tone of voice and take the time to script out notes for calls I need to make.

Conversely, don't be afraid to be human in less formal sessions. In work meetings, set the conditions for people to follow your lead and be themselves. I truly believe that people do their best work when they can be close to their authentic selves, and as a Project Manager, it's easy to be seen as an outsider telling people what to do and when to do it.

Add Value

Finally, always bring recommendations. In my experience, the greatest diminisher of confidence is the act of throwing a proverbial office grenade into an Oversight Group and sitting back to watch the fallout. Projects come with problems, some of them unexpected. You don't own them, and they aren't your fault. But the Customer is looking to you for confidence that the problem can be solved. If raising a problem within a project, follow the principle of communicating honestly. Understand it, assess it, challenge it, and make recommendations, including what the immediate actions should be. Remember, these problems would still exist if you weren't there. The aim isn't to have no problems; the aim is to ensure that you inspire confidence in the project team when those problems arise. And that your Customer can sleep soundly knowing that even though there is an issue, they have you managing it.

In Conclusion

When buried deep in the workings of a complex project, it's easy to focus solely on what you are doing and forget how you are doing it. And in a role where personal perception plays such a significant role, maintaining confidence in the project and your ability to manage it can mean the difference between success and failure. It's critical to ensure that you not only do the job well but are seen to be doing the job well.

Chapter 11

Protect, Serve, and Challenge

Executing projects is difficult. At least, it requires a lot of effort from a lot of people. That effort comes amid a time of significant change and uncertainty, as well as a sense of heightened scrutiny from those who want to see the project delivered. The project team is comprised of individuals with varying skills, experience, and personalities. What motivates and demotivates will change from person to person, as will the way they manage the conditions within the project. Those people are often likely to feel under-appreciated, over-worked, and sometimes disillusioned.

As we established in *Chapter 3*, the role of the Leader is to maintain optimal performance of a project team throughout the project, and the success of a Leader is judged by the cumulative output of the team they manage. The first two roles of a Project Manager (The Consultant, The Planner) are mainly technical in nature. They require consultation and collaboration with others but also significant output from you as an individual. Once you move into the Execution phase, the Leadership role takes precedence, and success in this role looks very different to its predecessors. While the other two roles are heavily focused on ensuring the Customer and other stakeholders have confidence in you, the Leader role extends that requirement out to the team doing the work within the project.

Defining how to perform as a Leader is more complicated than it is for the Consultant and Planner roles, and far more subjective. The impact of not performing the role well will take longer to materialise, but the consequences will be just as severe. As we know from The Hierarchy of Operational Excellence, the people doing the work have the greatest impact on your project delivery, making this a fundamental challenge to address.

Maintaining a team that operates at optimal performance for the duration of the project requires an approach I like to think of as 'protect, serve, and challenge'. This works on the basis that the project team have three fundamental requirements of a Project Manager.

1. **Protection**
   To be isolated from the demands and pressures of external sources.

2. **Service**
   To have the environmental conditions for high performance established and maintained throughout the project.

3. **Challenge**
   To ensure that a clear direction of travel is maintained, together with a healthy challenge to perform and develop.

In my experience, it's common for Project Managers to take a task-oriented approach to project execution, a style of management I call 'The Hammer'. By this I mean tracking execution against plan and adopting a somewhat ruthless approach to deviation: driving execution at all costs. While this can produce results in the short term, those results come at the cost of long-term performance. Effective leadership means having a box full of tools and the skill and nuance to know which tool to apply for any given situation (and by the way, sometimes 'The Hammer' is actually needed!).

So, alongside the hard skills, the behaviours required for being an effective Leader are as follows (in no particular order):

Bring the energy

Apathy is a silent killer of projects. Most projects have a lengthy delivery time. They take a lot of work, often involve ambitious deadlines, and have regularly changing priorities. Combined, these factors can have a negative impact on the morale of the team. As a Project Manager, you'll lead most of the calls and interactions with the team, and it is crucial you bring energy to those interactions. Projects are hard work but should be rewarding for those involved. They are a privilege to work on and present a significant opportunity for development. As a Leader it is important to set the tone, to bring energy, bring humour, and bring honesty to the team. Be the energy you want the team to have. The team will look to you, consciously and unconsciously, for confidence. If apathy is a silent project killer, then prevention must become a daily task.

Be the idiot in the room

Ambiguity is the enemy of execution. Left unchallenged it can eat away at your team's confidence in themselves, you, and the project overall. The only way to remove ambiguity is to challenge it, to seek clarification. But your team will be made up of a wide range of people. People from various teams, with various skill sets. Some will be internal employees, while some may be from other organisations. Some permanent, some contractors. And within those groups, individuals are likely to have a wide variety of backgrounds and personalities. All those variables combined can have a major influence on an individual's ability to vocalise a concern they may have. A single employee working on a critical piece of work who is not confident with what's required of them can be a problem. Multiply that across an entire project team and there's a strong chance your project will be derailed.

Combine ambiguity with an organisation's love for the use of jargon and you potentially compound the problem even further, particularly if the organisation has a culture that is less than open to challenge. The impact of ambiguity may appear obvious: a project team member misunderstands a deliverable, spends time working on it, only to deliver something other than what was required. But ambiguity can result in a wider, more systemic problem: the medium-to-long-term depletion of confidence. The establishment of a culture where people feel passively discouraged from asking questions allows the seeds of doubt to be sown, and this can eat away at the foundations of team cohesion.

Even the most outspoken person can succumb to social pressures to conform. To not stand out from the crowd or risk embarrassment. I regularly meet people out with their dogs and often ask the name of the dog without asking the name of the owner. If I fail to ask their name at the second meeting, I risk building up a psychological barrier where it becomes too awkward to ask their name, for risk of embarrassment. It's this same awkward (but not malicious) pressure that can impact an individual's confidence to question something they don't understand.

As a team leader, it's your responsibility to not only actively remove ambiguity and jargon from your project but to also set the conditions where others feel comfortable, possibly obliged, to raise questions and concerns the moment they have them. And the simplest and most effective approach to encourage this is to lead by example. Demonstrating the behaviour yourself and establishing a safe culture of curiosity will show team members that it can be done, and without negative consequences. Be the idiot in the room. Ask the stupid questions. Make it clear that you know it's a stupid question, but you feel it's important to get clarity for your own benefit. This effectively sets a new baseline for the team to operate within. It sets the tone and says this type of behaviour is acceptable and encouraged. More importantly, if your team start to model it themselves, they may just be developing a behaviour that benefits them for the rest of their career.

Be the calm voice in the storm
As Project Managers, we operate within the continuous turbulence of change. Being comfortable with a changing

environment is a pre-requisite for the role, but often this isn't the case for experts working within a project team. Many of them may be suspicious of the intentions of the project to begin with and may not be as resilient to working in uncertain circumstances. We have a duty as Project Managers to be sympathetic to these individuals and act as a buffer between the team and the wider environment.

Having a Project Manager should mean that team members are able to work in a safe environment, one where they can focus on their immediate tasks and on supporting the wider project team. That doesn't mean hiding things from the team. It means removing the drama from any communications. Removing the oxygen from potential speculation and gossip and treating the project team as responsible adults and professionals.

I've worked on many projects where team members are temporary contract workers, some by choice, some by necessity. Some have young families and, as such, are particularly sensitive to the shock of potential job insecurity. Changes, or even rumours of changes, can cause individuals significant distress, given the potential impact on their family. This is completely understandable and completely predictable. At a Project Management level, it causes an unnecessary impact on productivity. At a human level, it's an unnecessarily uncomfortable situation for someone to navigate. Foster an environment where the team knows they can come to you for clarification and where they trust you to come to them with information they need to know.

Lead by serving

As with many other disciplines, the challenge of leading a team can drive the wrong behaviour in some individuals. Often with good intentions, many Project Managers misinterpret what it means to lead people. One of the most common mistakes is attempting to assert authority over the team for authority's sake – the misconception that control over a team is key and compliance is the aim. This militaristic approach has its place when compliance is necessary, such as when people are required to override their natural instincts and follow orders even in the face of danger. In this case, the Leader is the master and following orders is the objective. I've yet to come across a project where this is needed.

A much better perspective is that work is the master and each member of the team is producing value through that work. As a Leader, I'm not the focus, the work is. I'm an engineer and my team are the engine, each member a piston. My job is to set the pace at which the engine can run to produce the most output over time and carefully tune the engine to ensure that output is maintained. When I see a piston start to misfire, my task is to detect it and adjust it to bring it back online. The sooner I spot the issue, the less likely it is to become misaligned. And if I continue to monitor, adjust, and maintain a pace that is sustainable, we have the best chance of producing the output that we need.

Alternatively, imagine your project team is only being paid for every minute of work they do that is related to specific project deliverables. In this scenario, protecting your team from unnecessary distractions would be essential to maximise time spent on what's important, and therefore, achieve the maximum profit. Serving your project team by removing any unnecessary work and distractions would give the maximum return for their time. Keeping your project team focused on the value work is critical, and a Leader's job is to constantly review how they can serve their team to help them focus on that task.

Play devil's advocate

Conflict resolution is a constant challenge throughout a project. The ability to challenge individuals, their ideas, and their behaviours is an essential skill, from Customer consultation to managing issues within the project team.

Dealing with conflict was something I had to learn. In my youth, I avoided conflict, or anything that I even considered conflict, much to the detriment of my own success and well-being. It wasn't that I thought situations would escalate into a physical altercation, or even that I was afraid of physical altercations. It was more that I lacked the confidence to even risk offending someone. And this was coupled with an overly sensitive perception of what offending someone might mean. This trait developed into what I would describe as a chronic appeasement syndrome. I always disliked the outcomes but was never 'brave' enough to prevent them from occurring.

At some point, I managed to come to terms with the issue and solve it forever. Through various less-than-pleasant outcomes, I learnt to identify the moments where I could 'feel' a potential conflict building. Maybe I could sense I was about to react, to avoid something, or maybe it was just something in the air. Either way, at those moments, I knew there were two possible outcomes. I could either face into a potential conflict and have a challenging conversation with someone, or I could avoid that conversation altogether and let a situation play out to a negative conclusion. Neither of these outcomes seemed good to me, but one of them was guaranteed to diminish my credibility. And in the end, the fear of losing credibility outweighed any other fear I had and meant I had to face into the potential conflict.

Over time, I learnt more. I realised that I viewed challenging a decision or an idea as in some way doubting or disrespecting the individual who suggested it. To work around this, I just needed to tell myself – and genuinely believe – that I wasn't being disrespectful. And the solution I landed on, and that has worked for me ever since, is to play devil's advocate. To be the person who puts in a challenge for the sake of the project, much like an academic peer review. The person who tries to ensure the project hypothesis is solid and that potentially critical issues are eliminated through robust challenge.

That simple shift in mindset changed everything, enabling me to challenge things I didn't understand, didn't agree with, or wasn't convinced was the right course of action. This wasn't me personally challenging another individual, it was me in my Project Manager role, robustly challenging potential issues in the name of quality assurance.

Set the direction, continuously

Being a Project Manager is a privileged position. Throughout the lifetime of a project, you will remain the most informed person in the entire organisation on each specific change. From the original concept and the thoughts and concerns of the organisational leaders, right through to the day-to-day workings of the project team, you will have more knowledge than any other individual. And with that privilege comes a related responsibility. The individuals in the project team will have a limited view of the overall project, which can make it difficult for them to understand their task or role within the wider project context. The proverbial lumberjack getting lost in the woods while cutting their own tree. The same can be said of the Customer and their Oversight Group, who receive fewer updates and manage larger-scale issues and may lose sight of the fundamentals of the project along the way.

As the Project Manager, it is your job to frequently reorient those working within the project. Take a moment at each oversight meeting to walk through the fundamentals (why? what? how? when? how much?) before going into detail.

Remind the project team of the wider objective they are working towards and what the immediate next step is. Reiterate how the task they are performing relates to the wider objective. Share your knowledge, set the direction, do it frequently, and keep it really, really simple. Remember that nobody within the project has as much information as you do.

Don't let moments turn into months

During execution there will be moments that test your trust in your instincts. Small moments where you feel there is a problem under the surface that hasn't yet emerged, making you question whether the problem is real or not. A team member giving a response that doesn't quite convince, individuals missing meetings without notification, or low attendance of meetings in general. Things that you feel are indicative of an unhealthy project but don't quite cross the threshold to warrant tackling head-on or escalating as potential issues for an Oversight Group.

In my experience, these moments matter. Rarely have I chosen to observe and monitor these situations and not regretted that choice. The more projects you run, the more sensitive you become to the early signs of larger issues within a project team or the project in general.

The key to tackling these issues effectively is to proactively establish, monitor, and report on project health statistics. At the start of the project, call out the metrics that you intend to monitor and formalise them. For example:

- **Meeting attendance**

Publish meeting attendance statistics from the start of your project. It's a great indicator of project engagement and sets the expectation from the start. It also provides a great conversation starter for individuals who you think may be falling below expectations on this point. It becomes a conversation regarding project health rather than a criticism of them as an individual.

- **Team morale**

You may not be managing a team directly within your project, but you are leading them. Feed back your subjective view of team health to your Customer and Oversight Group. Establish a regular check-in point with team members (and their line manager if it's not you). Having this in place before issues arise gives you an opportunity to discuss specific concerns without making them seem like a big issue. It also allows team members who may be less vocal in group settings to voice their thoughts and questions.

- **Task tracking**

Tracking against plan is something that should be done as standard within all projects. It's a core element of understanding whether your project is aligned with its original time prediction. This is normally done at a high level against the project plan with the Customer. However, at least in the early stages, I'm a huge fan of producing some simple statistics around the detailed level of task execution. What percentage of 'sub-tasks' have not been completed on their planned date? How many have been missed? Here's an example of a task with its sub-tasks (with the sub-tasks in reverse sequence):

- **Paint the Living Room (main task)**
  - **Sand walls (sub-task)**
  - **Fill holes/dents (sub-task)**
  - **Cover flooring (sub-task)**
  - **Purchase materials (sub-task)**

'Paint the Living Room' would generally be the level of task I would report to a Customer. Discussions at the sub-task level would usually be with the project team – though reporting on the performance of sub-tasks more widely early in the project can give a useful indication of execution health, and again, is great for conversations with the team.

In Conclusion

Being an effective Leader isn't easy. It falls firmly into the art of Project Management and takes time to master. As a simple, useful exercise, take a moment to think about great leaders you have worked with in the past. Write down five characteristics that made them stand out in your mind. What did they do for you? What did they do that others couldn't or wouldn't? How many of those behaviours align with the themes above?

The Mindset Tips
General

Chapter 12

Build Your Customer's House

Throughout this book, I've tried to emphasise the importance of understanding the 'why'. The reason I focus on mindset over methodology is simple. If you understand the concepts of change in their simplest form, where they originated, and what problems they were designed to solve, then you'll find them easier to apply.

Conversely, learning just the methodology, which steps to follow, which tools to use, leaves you at the risk of encountering problems for the first time without the agility to determine the correct approach to solving them. Within the methodology of Project Management, the roles, the documentation, the terminology, it's easy to get distracted from the core purpose. And so you perform the steps at the cost of keeping the wider project on course. But like learning to play songs on a piano by memorising which keys to press without learning how to read music, the range and flexibility of your performance is limited.

When feeling lost in the detail of a project, my advice to new Project Managers is to frame any issue in a way that is as relatable and tangible as possible. Whenever I coach or mentor someone, I recommend equating your project to that of building a house. Most people have had experience of undertaking some kind of house renovation at some point in their lives. You may be fortunate enough to have had a house built or renovated a house you own. At the very least, you've likely lived in a house being renovated or even had a family member who works in a construction trade. If so, referencing the practical challenges of these experiences can help translate a challenge in your current project into a more relatable example.

Let's use a common example for 'office-based' projects: resourcing. Many organisations fail to appreciate the importance of dedicating sufficient resources to large-scale projects. While they realise resources are required, it is often assumed that people can perform multiple roles, and so resources are allocated based on a percentage of their time. For example, allocating a software developer 50% to your project and 50% to another. In a resource model, this may appear manageable, but the overhead and inefficiency of that resource split is mostly invisible 'on paper'. The time required to put down one piece of work and pick up work on a previous project is significant. Conflicting priorities and timelines mean missed meetings, requiring additional time with others in the project to catch up. Being unavailable for immediate, ad-hoc project meetings to discuss pressing issues restricts project flexibility and may prevent others from progressing with their work. These inefficiencies are difficult to quantify, and hard to appreciate by someone looking solely at costs and resource models.

Now let's translate that to the house building example. Imagine suggesting that a bricklayer split their time between your current house build and another. A bricklayer's scheduling is one of the most predictable in the project plan. The number of bricks per day is a relatively steady metric to estimate, and the levels of the build can be planned in accordance to allow other trades to schedule their time in advance. Roofers have a good idea about a predicted start date and constant visibility of progress. Window fitters are also able to initiate their longer-tail timelines once the window brickwork has been completed.

Now imagine splitting the same bricklayer 50% between two different house builds. Not only is the number of bricks laid per day on an individual site halved, but bricklaying time is immediately lost because of the travelling between sites. Time may need to be spent on the last day at the first site to transport and secure materials and tools. Time may need to be spent on arrival at each site to become familiar with any changes to the planned build while they were at the other site. In addition, the absence of the bricklayer on one particular site may be preventing other trades from resolving issues where clarification is required from the bricklayer. And finally, the split in time would ultimately mean that both builds would take at least twice the amount of time. This extends the window for risks to materialise and prevents other activities (roofing, windows) from starting, which may then have a downstream impact on other timelines.

The house-building example helps illustrate the importance of sequencing and dependencies – the order in which tasks need to happen, who needs to do them, and which tasks cannot start or complete without others being started or completed. In a software development example, the task flexibility may be greater as software delivery can be packaged into smaller components or developed in an Agile fashion. This may mean sequencing becomes less linear and makes direct lines of dependency less clear. If a developer is unable to start one component, they may be able to move on to a component elsewhere, giving more flexibility and effectively disguising sequencing issues. In the house-building example, dependency issues become more apparent. If your expected delivery of bricks is delayed by two days but your bricklayer has arrived on site as agreed, you have a person physically on site who cannot work, still needing to be paid, and two days' bricklaying work that has very obviously not happened. Similarly, if you fail to identify dependencies correctly, you may have contractors arrive who are unable to progress. For example, being unable to enter a house because a concrete floor hasn't dried.

The house building example – the full project cycle

Let's take a look at a more complete example. As a customer (in the UK in this instance), you start with a vision of building a house. You might have a clear idea of what you want. You work with an architect who reviews your brief, challenges it, uses qualifications and experience to determine what's possible, drafts high-level plans for the house, and packages it up for approval. High-level build cost estimates are provided.

These plans are then submitted for local planning approval. Local residents are consulted, and objections are lodged. An approval decision is made, and the project either stops here or continues.

If it continues, the architect then produces detailed building specifications that provide the specific deliverables for the house build: the construction method, the material types, and the technical tolerances. This effectively forms the acceptance criteria for the final build. Again, this is submitted for approval.

We can consider this period to be the initial **Consultation Stage**.

At a simple level, the Customer has taken their high-level idea, worked with a **Consultant** to detail what outcome they want, with indicative costs giving an initial view on the Customer's **willingness to proceed**. The approval stage with the planner also gives an early checkpoint on the Customer's **ability to proceed**. In methodology terms, this would align with the **Initiation Stage** of the project.

Once approved, the Customer then seeks a builder and a Project Manager. In most cases, a building contractor will perform both roles. The builder takes the plans and the specifications and provides an overall estimate and timeline for the build. If a fully finished house is expected, then more detailed discussions are held that provide full detail. For example, bathroom design, flooring type, fixtures and fittings, and landscaping. A staged approach to the build is defined, highlighting the funding stages the Customer must meet to continue the build. The staged approach is reviewed, and if agreed, a contract is drawn up detailing the terms of the agreement. This agreement is then sent to the Customer for approval.

At this point, we have crossed into the **Planner** role, with detailed deliverables defined, detailed cost and time estimates provided, and success criteria agreed for both the deliverables and the overall project. Resource requirements have been defined, stages of delivery have been defined, and a method of engagement has been agreed. This would align with the **Planning Stage** in Project Management methodologies.

If the Customer agrees and signs the contract, the project is resourced. Sub-contractors (electricians, plumbers, window fitters, etc.) are assigned, and each is given detailed tasks to complete the build, along with the specifications required to do so successfully. The tasks are sequenced by the builder in logical order. Each sub-contractor in this case could be seen as a workstream lead, with some of them having multiple people working in their specific area to help complete the task. In the case of a house build managed by the builder with sub-contractors who are regularly used, there may not be a detailed project plan. Given the repeat nature of most house builds, it may be taken for read that the sequencing of the tasks is well understood amongst the team.

Project Execution then progresses with each sub-contractor working to complete their individual tasks and working under the guidance of the builder. The builder and the Customer regularly check in to monitor progress, discuss issues, and make any decisions that are needed. Whether formally or informally, an **Oversight Group** has been established. Building control officers have regular inspections scheduled to ensure the building meets regulations. The Customer's family are likely to be involved in making decisions as they have a vested interest in the final outcome. The architect may also need to be informed and consulted during the build to ensure the building is completed to the original plans.

The builder is acting as the **Leader** through the **Execution Stage**, ensuring contractors are meeting their obligations, dealing with issues on site, and managing issues and risks that could pose future problems for the build.

And finally, the build is handed over. The Customer inspects and agrees that the build has met their contractual agreements before releasing the final payment. This would be considered **Project Closure**.

Through this lens, Project Management becomes less complex. The fundamental risks and complexities that require some discipline to avoid are obvious. The potential for budget overrun and time delays is front and centre. The need to seek approval from the Customer (and others) at critical stages before proceeding is logical, along with the requirement to define and agree detailed deliverables with the Customer and agree the criteria that would define success for each one.

In Conclusion

While the mostly repeatable nature of most 'standard' domestic house builds means they don't necessarily require a dedicated Project Manager, they do provide a tangible example of Project Management in practice. So, if you find yourself struggling with how to approach a specific concept within a project, try relating it back to building a house. Life on a building site is conceptually simple. The objectives are clear, progress is visible, issues become rapidly apparent, and sequencing is critical. If you feel your current project isn't as easily explained, try addressing the basics.

Chapter 13

Programmes Are Just Really Big Projects

The terms 'project' and 'programme' are used regularly but often misunderstood. I'd go further. They are a source of confusion and potential loss of confidence for new Project Managers.

While editing this book, I spent some time deliberating over whether it was even worth covering the difference between projects and programmes. It's far from being the most significant challenge facing Project Managers, and the impact of the issue is relatively small. But it's an issue that has always bothered me because it's a perfect example of the industry introducing unnecessary, complex nomenclature for the benefit of absolutely nobody.

So, what do we mean by a programme and a project? And what does a Programme Manager do differently from a Project Manager? I've heard various definitions and explanations for this including: projects deliver products, programmes deliver outcomes. An interesting perspective.

A blog posted on **PRINCE2.com** suggests:

> "A **project** is a unique and temporary organisation, designed to deliver a tangible output. It has a fixed – generally fairly short – timeframe, and a project manager is responsible for delivering the output on time and on budget ... A **programme** is the coordinated management of a number of related projects and other activities. The purpose of a programme is to deliver a strategic outcome and organisational benefit. Programmes are generally long

term. Because the specific deliverables may not be fully defined at the start, a programme will often have a broad, adaptable scope. In short, a programme consists of several projects."

The Association for Project Management has a similar definition, describing it in terms of a mission to the moon (with the rocket build being a project and the mission to the moon being the programme).

Conceptually, I see what both definitions are saying, particularly how a programme can be seen as the management of multiple projects. But experience has taught me that there is no fundamental difference between them – or that the difference between them is smaller than the confusion introduced by the terminology. In effect, it's just a conversation about two key points:

1. **Perspective**
   What level of detail do you need to see in your project? What do you need to plan and track to effectively execute the plan and achieve your outcome?

2. **Scale**
   What size does a project need to be for you to insert dedicated Change Management professionals to effectively manage it?

The issue here is the subjectivity around who determines what a project is. In other words, one person's deliverable is another person's project. Or one person's project is another's programme.

Let's take a look in a bit more detail.

Using our Customer's house
To build our Customer's house, we employ a Project Manager to oversee the delivery. That Project Manager has a project team consisting of experts responsible for delivering the individual components required to complete the house. For example, an architect, builder, carpenter, electrician, plumber, kitchen fitter, landscape gardener. We call this a 'project'. The Project Manager works with the team to define a plan, where those deliverables are defined. Each deliverable will be something along the lines of (in very simplistic terms):

- **The outer walls**
- **The roof**
- **Plumbing and heating**
- **Electrical wiring**
- **Completed kitchen**
- **Completed garden**

Each of these deliverables has individual tasks and defined success criteria.

To most people, that feels sensible and like a standard project. But let's change the perspective a little. Imagine the garden is large, and the Customer wants some complex items included. A pool, a koi pond, a summer house, etc. The landscaping company may, quite rightly, consider this a project in isolation. They have a defined outcome, specific deliverables, a budget, a timeline, and criteria to work to. They are likely to have several people working on this and may also introduce sub-contractors or other suppliers to manage some of the deliverables. This may require a separate consultation to help clarify details before proceeding. But if we call the garden a project, does that render the overall house build a programme? Does the Project Manager suddenly become a Programme Manager? And does the house build project change? I don't think it does. What we call it is irrelevant. The real question is what conditions are required to give it the greatest chance of success. Particularly:

- **Perspective**
  At what level of detail do we want to track the landscaping actions on the parent house build project plan? To feel comfortable that we are executing well, do we want to see all the tasks required for all the deliverables in the garden? Or are we happy to leave that to the landscaping company to manage and track the higher-level garden delivery?
- **Scale**
  What level of complexity does there need to be – and how many people – to warrant having a Project Manager to focus on the garden? At what scale does it require its own Oversight Group?

Now let's assume a company intends to build a small estate of houses, such as a cul-de-sac, with five houses to be built.

Assume that each house is complex enough to require its own Project Manager and that the Customer could choose to hire five different Project Managers and work with each of them individually to progress each project. Even if the Customer has the will, this would require a lot of time and focus from them – and from their Oversight Group – to work with multiple Project Managers. The alternative would be to hire someone to oversee the overall delivery, effectively making it a programme. The overall outcome is defined as the completion of the five individual projects, and the Programme Manager works with the Customer and the Oversight Group to deliver this.

For the Customer and Programme Manager, the perspective shifts. Project Managers become workstream leads from the programme perspective. House builds now become deliverables of a programme rather than projects. From a governance perspective, the Programme Manager adds another layer of management that was previously not required. A role that doesn't deliver specific deliverables but that now becomes necessary to manage the managers and coordinate the delivery of the overall outcome. Without the additional layer, the Customer loses the benefit of Project Management, and the Project Managers lack the coordination to achieve the overall outcome.

An issue of magnification
A method I like to use to illustrate the point is picturing a high-powered telescope positioned in space, pointing towards Earth, and you have the controls. When looking at the planet,

you see the complexity of the entire globe. The oceans, the rainforests, the mountains. A global level of complexity. At night, you get a simple illuminated view of countries and cities, but at a very low level of detail.

You then zoom in to an individual continent and start to see country-level detail. Individual elements of land relief, different cities, and roads. A whole layer of complexity not previously visible. As you continue to zoom down to city level, you start to highlight people. Millions of them, previously invisible, their houses, their vehicles, moving around in complex patterns. You continue to a single house, and you see a fully self-contained, functioning system. The routine of a complex family life, the food they eat, the pets they have. Effectively, the level of complexity remains, but the scale of the individual items becomes smaller.

If you continue to zoom in, you start to discover insects, an ant nest, equally complex, but at a much smaller scale. This can be continued down to an atomic level, where individual atoms are performing highly complex chemical activity that the human eye or even an insect eye cannot begin to detect. This layered level of complexity is present within projects. Even a single task on a project plan can consist of a series of extremely complex steps, possibly even for more than one individual.

Now imagine you have been given access to the telescope and tasked with reporting on global cloud patterns on a daily basis. Zoomed out to planetary level, this would be possible for an individual. But now imagine being asked to report on daily weather patterns at a country level. This would mean monitoring individual continents throughout the day, possibly individual countries, a level of detail that would be too much for one person to monitor. And it would need a closer perspective. At this point, more people would be required to do the same job but at a more detailed level. The tasks performed are the same, but more individuals with the same skills are required to do it.

In Conclusion

Examples such as these help to bring some clarity to the project vs. programme debate. In my opinion, there are no programmes, just bigger projects. The larger they get, the further away the Customer needs to be from the detail to maintain effective oversight. But the level of detail involved doesn't change, so as the project grows, the more change professionals are needed within the project to break it into effective, manageable pieces. And while you would still want your most experienced Project Managers as high up the pyramid as possible for maximum impact, what they are called is irrelevant.

Final Thoughts

Throughout this book I have tried to emphasise some key themes. That people are more important than processes, that being a good Project Manager is more than simply knowing how to manage projects, and that the mindset of a Project Manager is more important than the methodology used. And while I believe all of those things are true, in no way do I wish to promote a message that is anti-methodology.

My stance on methodologies is complicated. While they are necessary and provide significant value, their push towards standardisation is not always helpful. PRINCE2, a methodology I have considerable experience of, is somewhat of a masterpiece. But it can also be extremely confusing as a starting point for someone entering the profession. And while there is very little within the framework to disagree with, I have seen few organisations with an appetite to follow it in its full form, despite its scalability.

And in keeping with the themes of this book, the issue doesn't lie with the methodology but with the people. There is a tendency to be dogmatic rather than pragmatic, to see methodologies as a silver bullet for the pain of delivering change. To adopt a methodology because of its reputation for success and then being either too impatient to follow it effectively or so rigid in applying it that it becomes impracticable. As people, we have a frustrating tendency to interpret methods in a way that minimises the benefits while maximising the disbenefits.

Of course, this doesn't only apply to Project Management methodologies. I've seen organisations adopt Agile as an organisation-wide development strategy, only to corporatise it, adopting all the terminology but adding layers of bureaucracy and removing any of the benefits Agile was intended to deliver - and is capable of delivering. I've worked for one of the largest corporations on the planet, famous for its success utilising Six Sigma, to then move directly into another business and industry where the same methodology was almost unmentionable because of some notorious failures within that sector. I've delivered cost-saving projects that have reduced spend by more than some sizeable organisations could hope to make in annual revenue, simply by undoing the negative effects of a process improvement methodology implemented as an ideology.

I know that all of the methodologies in question *do* work. I've used them myself and have seen others use them to great success. But they are processes, and people are more important than processes. Or as we learnt earlier in the book, you can't solve a people problem with a process. Processes are tools to help people achieve something, but they can't solve a problem on their own.

The people using the tools need to understand them in depth in order to use them effectively. And the key to using them effectively is pragmatism: knowing not only which tool to use for the situation you are working in but also to what extent to deploy them for optimal effect. Knowing how strictly or widely you utilise the methodology for the type and size of your project is just as important as understanding how and when to apply it. And a key part of this decision is dependent on the industry. Let me explain.

My background and experience is mostly within Financial Services, an industry that operates in a strange environment of heavy regulation, significant scale, historical ways of working, and a desire to capitalise on opportunities quickly. This creates an interesting dilemma for Project Managers. On the one hand, methodologies are deeply embedded, and they are visible - to demonstrate strong operational risk practices to regulatory bodies. On the other hand, there is a mentality and culture where individuals make bold decisions quickly (although this varies greatly culturally across varying regions). Many organisations have simple products that have been sold for decades, sometimes centuries, and this can occasionally lead to a reluctance to embrace change and frustration at what they perceive to be complicated change processes. This means that for some projects, methodologies are delivered with a 'lighter touch' for the Customer and project team, while ensuring the full process is adhered to for the regulator. A less-than-ideal approach.

This dichotomy, this desire to appear to be doing what works rather than doing what actually works, perfectly highlights the challenge for Project Managers. We feel compelled to follow a methodology because it's expected, even if a significant amount of the work done is somewhat redundant. This highlights the importance of focusing on the elements that make a difference, on pragmatism over perfection. And while influencing this behaviour is not always within an individual Project Manager's control, it is sometimes necessary to explicitly question an organisation's appetite for process compliance. Doing so can help set a level of governance that is appropriate to the environment. It can also help introduce a mindset that says perfection isn't always required.

The appetite for process compliance varies greatly among industries. For example, in the early 2000s, technology companies developed a culture focused more on speed, experimentation, and 'failing fast'. Many of these were capital-rich and were pushing new boundaries in an environment where being first meant potentially being market leading. Telling the likes of Google or Apple that they had to fully apply a Project Management methodology for their new software platform would likely see you exiting the company by the time you'd finished your first sentence. Conversely, the thought of constructing a new nuclear power facility without an extreme amount of quality assurance would be insanity. Project Management methodologies help provide oversight and control to a complex delivery. But how strictly an organisation adheres to a methodology depends on its appetite for risk and on the environment in which the project exists. If a software product fails to do what it was intended to do for the organisation, this may have what seem like severe consequences. However, compared to the potential consequences of a large civil engineering project failing, they are likely to be less significant.

And that message of pragmatism is how I'd like to conclude this book. A successful Project Manager needs to know not only how to manage projects but also how to perform the roles of a Project Manager. They need to ascertain and be able to propose a level of project governance that is appropriate for the given project and the context in which it is being run. And while times have changed and technology has evolved, the project challenges most Project Managers will face in their careers are likely to be no more remarkable or complex than those encountered during the construction of the Hoover Dam

References

PRINCE2
Axelos website
axelos.com
Project Definition
axelos.com/certifications/prince2/what-is-project-management
Project Management Definition
axelos.com/certifications/prince2/what-is-project-management
Projects vs Programmes
prince2.com/uk/blog/project-vs-programme

Project Management Institute (PMI)
PMI website
pmi.org
Project Definition
pmi.org/about/what-is-a-project
Project Management Definition
pmi.org/about/what-is-project-management
Project Manager Definition
pmi.org/about/what-is-a-project-manager
PMBOK Guide
pmi.org/standards/pmbok

The Association for Project Management
APM website

apm.org.uk
Project Definition
apm.org.uk/resources/glossary/#p
Project Management Definition
apm.org.uk/resources/what-is-project-management
Project Manager Definition
apm.org.uk/resources/glossary/#p

International Project Management Association (IPMA)
ipma.world

The Second Industrial Revolution
en.wikipedia.org/wiki/Second_Industrial_Revolution

The Principles of Scientific Management
en.wikipedia.org/wiki/The_Principles_of_Scientific_Manage
ment

The Ford Assembly Line
corporate.ford.com/articles/history/moving-assembly-
line.html

Toyota Production System
en.wikipedia.org/wiki/Toyota_Production_System

Total Quality Management
en.wikipedia.org/wiki/Total_quality_management

Six Sigma
en.wikipedia.org/wiki/Six_Sigma

The Waterfall Method

en.wikipedia.org/wiki/Waterfall_model

The Agile Manifesto

agilemanifesto.org

Henry Gantt

en.wikipedia.org/wiki/Henry_Gantt

Hoover Dam

en.wikipedia.org/wiki/Hoover_Dam

Critical Path Method (CPM)

en.wikipedia.org/wiki/Critical_path_method

Program Evaluation and Review Technique

en.wikipedia.org/wiki/Program_evaluation_and_review_technique

Acknowledgements and Thanks

The biggest thank you to my wife Jo, for providing not only the reason, but also the encouragement to take a chance.

Thank you to Paddy Hartnett (www.paddyhartnett.com) without whose detailed eye, concise phrasing, and encouraging words, this book would have fallen far short of the quality I intended.

And to Anne Steel at Maui Waui Design (www.mauiwauidesign.co.uk) for the masterful cover art and logo design. For having the rare ability to consistently translate the vaguest of briefs into the most impactful artwork.

And a huge thank you to the many dedicated professionals I've had the pleasure of working with over the years. I've learnt so much from so many and hope to have passed at least a little on to others along the way.

About the Author

Ian Juniper is a seasoned change professional with over twenty years of experience delivering organisational change for FTSE100 and Fortune 500 companies within the Financial Services and the Oil & Gas industries. Passionate about delivering change that matters and developing the next generation of Project Managers, Ian offers Consultancy, Delivery, Training, and Coaching services through his independent consultancy The Pragmatic Professional. www.pragmaticprofessional.com

Index

Agile, 4, 29, 30, 36, 137, 153, 159

APM, 11, 13, 14, 157

Behaviours, 4, 36, 43, 45, 51, 52, 53, 56, 61, 64, 66, 122, 127, 132

Change Management, 36, 145

Closure, 15, 141

Consultant, 6, 52, 61, 72, 73, 75, 76, 79, 83, 85, 87, 120, 139

CPM, 31, 159

Customer, 15, 18, 19, 21, 24, 52, 53, 57, 63, 64, 65, 66, 67, 68, 69, 70, 72, 73, 74, 75, 76, 77, 78, 79, 83, 85, 86, 89, 91, 95, 98, 99, 101, 104, 105, 113, 114, 116, 118, 120, 127, 129, 131, 132, 134, 139, 140, 141, 146, 148, 150, 154

Deliverable(s), 10, 12, 15, 19, 22, 23, 36, 55, 56, 83, 86, 104, 105, 106, 107, 108, 109, 115, 123, 127, 139, 140, 141, 145, 146, 147, 148

Execution, 15, 18, 56, 58, 61, 105, 120, 140, 141

Fundamentals, 9, 24, 69, 75, 77, 88, 129

Gantt Chart, 30

Hoover Dam, 30, 37, 156, 159

IPM, 2

IPMA, 2, 31, 158

Lean, 27, 36

Methodology, 1, 2, 3, 4, 6, 14, 20, 24, 26, 28, 32, 34, 36, 48, 51, 64, 83, 135, 139, 140, 152, 153, 154, 155

Mindset, 1, 2, 5, 6, 49, 51, 55, 58, 62, 64, 84, 85, 87, 93, 94, 98, 111, 114, 128, 133, 135, 152, 155

Operational Excellence, 36, 40, 42, 47, 48, 99, 121

Oversight Group, 15, 18, 21, 24, 57, 69, 90, 99, 105, 118, 129, 130, 131, 141, 147, 148

People, 5, 23, 39, 40, 41, 42, 46, 47, 48, 49, 104, 123

PERT, 31

Planner, 120, 140

Planning, 15, 56, 61, 83, 140

PMBOK, 31, 32, 157

PMI, 2, 10, 12, 14, 31

PRINCE2, 2, 4, 10, 12, 13, 32, 36, 144, 152, 157

Processes, 1, 5, 12, 13, 14, 27, 30, 36, 39, 40, 41, 42, 44, 45, 46, 47, 48, 49, 83, 152, 153, 154

Programme Manager, 144, 147, 148

Programme(s), 143, 144, 145, 146, 147, 148, 150, 157

Project, 1, 2, 3, 4, 5, 6, 9, 10, 11, 12, 14, 15, 18, 19, 20, 21, 22, 23, 24, 30, 31, 36, 40, 48, 49, 51, 52, 53, 54, 55, 56, 57, 58, 59, 61, 64, 65, 66, 67, 68, 69, 70, 72, 73, 74, 75, 76, 77, 78, 79, 80, 81, 82, 83, 85, 86, 87, 88, 89, 90, 91, 92, 97, 98, 99, 100, 101, 102, 104, 105, 108, 113, 114, 115, 116, 118, 120, 121, 122, 123, 124, 125, 126, 127, 128, 129, 130, 131, 132, 135, 136, 138, 139, 140, 142, 144, 145, 146, 147, 148, 149, 150, 154, 155, 156, 157, 158

Project Charter, 67

Project Failure, 72

Project Initiation, 14

Project Management, 1, 2, 1, 2, 4, 5, 6, 8, 9, 10, 11, 12, 13, 14, 23, 24, 30, 31, 32, 36, 40, 48, 49, 51, 61, 65, 69, 72, 73, 74, 85, 89, 96, 97, 100, 101, 113, 125, 132, 135, 140, 141, 142, 145, 148, 153, 155, 157, 158

Project Manager, 2, 1, 3, 5, 6, 11, 13, 14, 15, 18, 20, 21, 23, 26, 37, 48, 49, 50, 51, 52, 55, 57, 61, 64, 65, 66, 67, 68, 69, 70, 74, 75, 76, 83, 85, 86, 87, 89, 90, 91, 96, 97, 98, 99, 100, 101, 102, 113, 117, 120, 121, 122, 125, 129, 139, 142, 144, 146, 147, 148, 152, 155, 156, 157, 158

Project Managers, 1, 2, 3, 4, 8, 9, 26, 51, 61, 64, 65, 71, 72, 74, 85, 86, 90, 98, 100, 121, 125, 126, 135, 144, 148, 150, 154, 156, 161

Project Success, 5, 72, 73, 74

Project Team, 14, 15, 23, 24, 40, 57, 58, 59, 64, 68, 76, 98, 99, 104, 113, 114, 115, 116, 118, 120, 121, 123, 125, 127, 129, 130, 132, 146, 154

Relationship, 65, 66, 67, 68, 69, 70, 85

Roles, 20, 50

Scope, 82, 83, 145

Scrum, 4, 30

Six Sigma, 4, 28, 36, 153, 158

Skills, 4, 5, 12, 13, 29, 36, 42, 43, 45, 51, 52, 53, 55, 56, 57, 58, 61, 64, 66, 88, 96, 97, 99, 101, 120, 122, 150

Stages, 9, 14, 15, 18, 19, 21, 23, 29, 58, 61, 76, 80, 86, 89, 105, 139, 140, 141

Steering Committee, 21, 24

Subject Matter Expert, 22
Sub-Stage, 18, 19, 23, 56, 57, 59
Systems, 40, 41, 42, 46, 47, 48, 49
The Consultant, 51, 52, 62, 120
The Leader, 51, 57, 111, 120, 141
The Planner, 51, 55, 94, 120
Toyota Production System, 27, 158
TQM, 28, 158
Waterfall, 29
Workstream Lead, 22, 23